RICE AND PEAS FOR THE SOUL 4

A THINK DOCTOR PUBLICATION

ISBN-13: 9781631733154

RASHADA

&

MAUD

COPYRIGHT NOTICE

ISBN-13: 9781631733154

ABOUT THE EDITOR

D. Constantine-Simms is an Occupational Psychologist and Counselling Psychologist and a qualified Therapeutic Career Coach, and regularly contributes to:

http://thinkdoctorcareercoaching.blogspot.co.uk

PAPERBACK BOOKS BY AUTHOR

Constantine-Simms has previously edited the following books:

- Rice & Peas For The Soul 2 (2015)
- Rice & Peas For The Soul 1 (2014)
- The Greatest Taboo: Homosexuality in Black Communities (2001)
- Hip Hop Had a Dream: Vol. 1 The Artful Movement (2008)

- 12 Years A Slave
- Behind The Scenes
- Thirty Years A Slave,...
- Incidents in the Life of a Slave...
- Fifty Years In Chains
- From Bondage To Freedom
- Hearts and Minds (Vol. 1)
- Hearts and Minds (Vol. 2)

E-BOOKS BY AUTHOR

- How to Get Motivated
- How to Plan For A New Career
- How to Develop Unstoppable Confidence
- Successful Interviews: Making The Most Of The Interview
- The Interview Guide: A Job Interview Is No Different Than Finding The Right Partner

- The Structure and Application of Cognitive Behavioural Therapy
- How to Think Critically
- Mentoring As A Workforce Development Strategy
- The Counselling Process In Six Stages: A Basic Guide For Psychologists Counsellors and Psychotherapists
- Linking Emotional Intelligence To Effective Leadership
- Stress Management
- A Critique Of Executive Coaching Through The Psychodynamic Window
- Otto Kernberg's Theory of Personality: Pathological Narcissism and Borderline Personality Disorders
- Personality Development and Confidence Building
- The Psychology of the Courtroom

- How To Improve Your Communication Skills
- How Employment Assessment Centres Work
- Effective Presentations Skills
- Linking Emotional Intelligence To Effective Leadership
- Stress Management Leading Career Development and Employability
- The History of Psychological Testing
- How To Have A Bad Interview
- Have You Ever Thought of Becoming A Life Coach
- Successful Interviews
- The 360 Degree Feedback System Is By Far The Best Performance Assessment Tool By Far.

CONTENTS

INTRODUCTION

One of my fondest memories as a child in the Caribbean is going by the river and sitting idly on the bank. There I would enjoy the peace and quiet, watch the water rush downstream, and listen to the chirps of birds and the rustling of leaves in the trees. I would also watch the bamboo trees bend under pressure from the wind and watch them return gracefully to their upright or original position after the wind had died down. When I think about the bamboo tree's ability to bounce back or return to its original position, the word resilience comes to mind. When used in reference to a person this word means the ability to readily recover from shock, depression or any other situation that stretches the limits of a person's emotions. Have you ever felt like you are about to snap? Have you ever felt like you are at your breaking point? Thankfully, you have survived the experience to live to talk about it. During the experience you probably felt a mix of emotions that threatened your health. You felt emotionally drained, mentally exhausted and you most likely endured unpleasant physical symptoms. Life is a mixture of good times and bad times, happy moments and unhappy moments. The next time you are experiencing one of those bad times or unhappy moments that take you close to your breaking point, bend but don't break. Try your best not to let the situation get the best of you. A measure of hope will take you through the unpleasant ordeal. With hope for a better tomorrow or a better situation, things may not be as bad as they seem to be. The unpleasant ordeal may be easier to deal with if the end result is worth having. If the going gets tough and you are at your breaking point, show resilience. Like the bamboo tree, bend, but don't break!

DIFFERENT TYPES OF GOALS THAT TAKE YOU TO SUCCESS

Leaders set goals. But they often set only one type of goal, and in so doing they set themselves up for failure. Here is the complete tool kit.

1) **Achievement goals** – These describe results that you will have when you finish the goal. Examples include: retire with a million dollars at age 65, earn a promotion by June, and increase sales by 5%. Most major goals are achievement goals.

2) **Action goals** – These describe specific actions that you will take to accomplish achievement goals. Examples include: meet with an investment counselor, attend a workshop to learn new job skills, contact all of the prospects in the database.

3) **Layered goals** – These specify the same goal with different levels of priority and difficulty. Example: Top Priority: Read one book each moth, Medium Priority: Read two books each month. Low Priority: Read three books each month. Use layered goals to stretch your performance beyond minimum achievements.

4) **Rate goals** – These specify actions repeatedly done over time. Examples include: Read two books per month, exercise three times per week, or write in a journal every day. Many personal growth activities can be performed as rate goals.

5) **Limit goals** – These set boundaries. Examples include: Spend less than $5,000 on new equipment, go to bed before 10 PM each night, and take less than 45 minutes for lunch while at work. These help manage priorities.

6) **Exclusion goals** – These state things that you will not do. Examples include: Do not watch TV after 8 P.M., do not use a cell

phone when with other people, do not eat junk foods. These help you decide in advance which activities you will avoid.

7) **Incredible goals** – These goals are highly optimistic, farfetched, or uncommonly aggressive. Examples include: Become CEO of a major corporation, write a best-selling novel, or win a Nobel Prize. These describe visions of ultimate success. If you set such goals, always supplement them with other more immediate and achievable goals that help you make progress toward these dreams.

THE SECRET OF SUCCESS!

A young man asked Socrates, an ancient Greek philosopher, the secret of Success. Socrates told the young man to meet him near the river the next morning. They met.

Socrates asked the young man to walk with him toward the river.

When the water got up to their necks, Socrates took the young man by surprise and ducked him into the water. The man struggled to get out but Socrates was strong and kept him under water until he started turning blue.

The young man struggled hard and finally managed to get up. The first thing he did was to gasp and take a deep breath.

Socrates asked, "What did you want the most when you were under the water?"
The man replied "Air".
Socrates said: "That's the most secret to success. When you want success as badly as you want air, you will get it. There is no other secret".

Reflection:

A burning desire is the starting point of all accomplishments. Just like a small fire cannot give much heat, a weak desire cannot produce great results…

SUCCESS DEPENDS UPON MATURITY!

Maturity is many things. It is the ability to base a judgment on the big picture, the long haul. It means being able to resist the urge for immediate gratification and opt for the course of action that will pay off later. One of the characteristics of the young is "I want it now."

Grown-up people can wait.

Maturity is perseverance–the ability to sweat out a project or a situation, in spite of heavy opposition and discouraging setbacks, and stick with it until it is finished. The adult who is constantly changing friends and changing mates is immature. He/she cannot stick it out because he/she has not grown up.

Maturity is the ability to control anger and settle differences without violence or destruction. The mature person can face unpleasantness, frustration, discomfort and defeat without collapsing or complaining. He/she knows he cannot have everything his/her own way every time. He/she is able to defer to circumstances, to other people- and to time. He/she knows when to compromise and is not too proud to do so.

Maturity is humility. It is being big enough to say, "I was wrong." And, when he/she is right, the mature person need not experience the satisfaction of saying, "I told you so."

Maturity is the ability to live up to your responsibilities, and this means being dependable. It means keeping your word. Dependability is the hallmark of integrity. Do you mean what you say-and do you say what you mean? Unfortunately, the world is filled with people who cannot be counted on. When you need them most, they are among the missing. They never seem to come through in the clutches. They break promises and substitute alibis for performance. They show up late or not at all.

They are confused and disorganized.
Their lives are a chaotic maze of broken promises, former friends, unfinished business and good intentions that somehow never materialize. They are always a day late and a dollar short.

ACRES OF DIAMONDS

One of the most interesting Americans who lived in the 19th century was a man by the name of Russell Herman Conwell. He was born in 1843 and lived until 1925. He was a lawyer for about fifteen years until he became a clergyman. One day, a young man went to him and told him he wanted a college education but couldn't swing it financially. Dr. Conwell decided, at that moment, what his aim in life was, besides being a man of cloth - that is. He decided to build a university for unfortunate, but deserving, students. He did have a challenge, however. He would need a few million dollars to build the university. For Dr. Conwell, and anyone with real purpose in life, nothing could stand in the way of his goal. Several years before this incident, Dr. Conwell was tremendously intrigued by a true story - with its ageless moral. The story was about a farmer who lived in Africa and through a visitor became tremendously excited about looking for diamonds. Diamonds were already discovered in abundance on the African continent and this farmer got so excited about the idea of millions of dollars' worth of diamonds that he sold his farm to head out to the diamond line. He wandered all over the continent, as the years slipped by, constantly searching for diamonds, wealth, which he never found. Eventually he went completely broke and threw himself into a river and drowned.

Meanwhile, the new owner of his farm picked up an unusual looking rock about the size of a country egg and put it on his mantle as a sort of curiosity.

A visitor stopped by and in viewing the rock practically went into terminal convulsions. He told the new owner of the farm that the funny looking rock on his mantle was about the biggest diamond that had ever been found. The new owner of the farm said, "Heck, the whole farm is covered with them" - and sure enough it was. The farm turned out to be the Kimberly Diamond Mine...the richest the world has ever known. The original farmer was literally standing on "Acres of Diamonds" until he sold his farm. Dr. Conwell learned from the story of the farmer and continued to teach it's moral. Each of us is right in the middle of our own "Acre of Diamonds", if only we would realize it and develop the ground we are standing on before charging off in search of greener pastures. Dr. Conwell told this story many times and attracted enormous audiences. He told the story long enough to have raised the money to start the college for underprivileged deserving students. In fact, he raised nearly six million dollars and the university he founded, Temple University in Philadelphia, has at least ten degree-granting colleges and six other schools.

When Doctor Russell H. Conwell talked about each of us being right on our own "Acre of Diamonds", he meant it. This story does not get old...it will be true forever...

Opportunity does not just come along - it is there all the time - we just have to see it.

SECRET SUCCESS STORIES

Have you read about the secret success stories? Here we will tell you one interesting story. A young man asked Socrates the secret to success. Socrates told the young man to meet him near the river the next morning .They met. Socrates asked the young man to walk with him toward the river. When the water got up to their neck, Socrates took the young man by surprise and ducked him into the water. The boy struggled to get out but Socrates was strong and kept him there until the boy started turning blue.

Socrates pulled his head out of the water and the first thing the young man did was to gasp and take a deep breath of air. Socrates asked:

" What did you want the most when you goal-setting? The boy replied: "Air." Socrates said: "That is the secret to success. When you want success as badly as you wanted the air, then you will get it. There is no other secret."

TAKE CONTROL OF MY LIFE

How to take control of my life? Perhaps a parable will help you see my point .take control of my life High on a hilltop overlooking the beautiful city of Venice, Italy, there lived an old man who was a genius. Legend had it he could answer any question anyone might ask of him. Two of the local boys figured they could fool the old man, so they caught a small bird and headed for his residence. One of the boys held the little bird in his hands and asked the old man if the bird was dead or alive. Without hesitation the old man said, "Son, if I say to you that the bird is alive, you will close your hands and crush him to death. If I say the bird is dead, you will open your hands and he will fly away. You see, son, in your hands you hold the power of life and death." In your hands you hold the seeds of failure or the potential for greatness. Your hands are capable but they must be used - and for the right things – to reap the rewards you are capable of attaining.

GROW GREAT BY DREAMS

The question was once asked of a highly successful businessman: "How have you done so much in your lifetime?" He replied, "I have dreamed. I have turned my mind loose to imagine what I wanted to do. Then I have gone to bed and thought about my dreams. In the night I dreamt about my dreams. And when I awoke in the morning, I saw the way to make my dreams real. While other people were saying, 'You can't do that, it isn't possible,' I was well on my way to achieving what I wanted." As Woodrow Wilson, 28th President of the U.S., said: "We grow great by dreams. All big men are dreamers." They see things in the soft haze of a spring day or in the red fire on a long winter's evening. Some of us let these great dreams die, but others nourish and protect them; nourish them through bad days until they bring them to the sunshine and light which comes always to those who sincerely hope that their dreams will come true. "So please, don't let anyone steal your dreams, or try to tell you they are too impossible. "Sing your song, dream your dreams, hope your hope and pray your prayer."

I CAN MAKE IT HAPPEN

History abounds with tales of experts who were convinced that the ideas, plans, and projects of others could never be achieved. However, accomplishment came to those who said, "I can make it happen." The Italian sculptor Agostino d'Antonio worked diligently on a large piece of marble. Unable to produce his desired masterpiece, he lamented, "I can do nothing with it." Other sculptors also worked this difficult piece of marble, but to no avail. Michelangelo discovered the stone and visualized the possibilities in it. His "I-can-make-it-happen" attitude resulted in one of the world's masterpieces - David.

The experts of Spain concluded that Columbus's plans to discover a new and shorter route to the West Indies was virtually impossible. Queen Isabella and King Ferdinand ignored the report of the experts. "I can make it happen," Columbus persisted. And he did. Everyone knew the world was flat, but not Columbus. The Nina, the Pinta, the Santa Maria, along with Columbus and his small band of followers, sailed to "impossible" new lands and thriving resources.

Even the great Thomas Alva Edison discouraged his friend, Henry Ford, from pursuing his fledgling idea of a motorcar. Convinced of the worthlessness of the idea, Edison invited Ford to come and work for him. Ford remained committed and tirelessly pursued his dream. Although his first attempt resulted in a vehicle without reverse gear, Henry Ford knew he could make it happen. And, of course, he did.

"Forget it," the experts advised Madame Curie. They agreed radium was a scientifically impossible idea. However, Marie Curie insisted, "I can make it happen."

Let's not forget our friends Orville and Wilbur Wright. Journalists, friends, armed forces specialists, and even their father laughed at the idea of an airplane. "What a silly and insane way to spend money. Leave flying to the birds," they jeered. "Sorry," the Wright brothers responded. "We have a dream, and we can make it happen." As a result, a place called Kitty Hawk, North Carolina, became the setting for the launching of their "ridiculous" idea.

Finally, as you read these accounts under the magnificent lighting of your environment, consider the plight of Benjamin Franklin. He was admonished to stop the foolish experimenting with lighting. What an absurdity and waste of time! Why, nothing could outdo the fabulous oil lamp. Thank goodness Franklin knew he could make it happen. You too can make it happen!

And she looked down into the well; and it was a happiness to see how the one became a blessing to the world, to see how much happiness and joy were felt everywhere. And she saw the other's life, and it was sorrow and distress, horror, and wretchedness.

"Both of them are God's will!" said Death.

"Which of them is Misfortune's flower and which is that of Happiness?" asked she.

"That I will not tell thee," said Death; "but this thou shalt know from me, that the one flower was thy own child! it was thy child's fate thou saw'st–thy own child's future life!"

Then the mother screamed with terror, "Which of them was my child? Tell it me! Save the innocent! Save my child from all that misery! Rather take it away! Take it into God's kingdom! Forget my tears; forget my prayers, and all that I have done!"

"I do not understand thee!" said Death. "Wilt thou have thy child again, or shall I go with it there, where thou dost not know!"

Then the mother wrung her hands, fell on her knees, and prayed to our Lord: "Oh, hear me not when I pray against Thy will, which is the best! hear me not! hear me not!" And she bowed her head down in her lap, and Death took her child and went with it into the unknown land.

FORGIVING THE KILLER OF MY PARENTS

Sue Norton lives in Arkansas City, Kansas. She received terrible news during a phone call from her brother in January 1990. Her much beloved, Daddy, Richard Denny and his wife Virginia were found murdered in their home. Sue's Daddy was shot to death in his isolated Oklahoma farmhouse. The crime netted the killer $17.00 and an old truck. Sue says she felt "numb". She couldn't understand why someone would want to hurt people who were old and poor. The loss of her Daddy just broke her heart.

Sue sat through the trial of Robert Knighton (B.K.). She was confused about how she should feel. She tells me that everyone in the courtroom was consumed with hate. They all expected her to feel the same way. But she couldn't hate the way they did because she says, "it didn't feel good."

The last night of the trial she knew there must be another way. She couldn't eat or sleep that night and prayed to God to help her. When morning came, she had this thought. "Sue, you don't have to hate B.K., you could forgive him".

The next day, while the jury was out for deliberation, Sue got permission to visit B.K. through the bars of his holding cell. Sue relates, "I was really frightened. This was my first experience in a jail. B.K. was big and tall; he was shackled and had cold steely eyes." At first B.K. refused to look at Sue. She asked him to turn around and he answered, "Why would anyone want to talk to me after what I have done?" Sue replied, "I don't know what to say to you. But I want you to know that I don't hate you. My grandmother always taught me not to use the word hate. She taught me that we are here to love one another. If you are guilty, I forgive you.. B.K. thought Sue was just playing games. He couldn't understand how she could forgive him for such a terrible crime. Sue says, "I didn't think of him as killer, I thought of him as a human being. People thought that Sue had lost her mind. Friends would step to the other side of the road to avoid her. But Sue says, "There is no way to heal and get over the trauma without forgiveness. You must forgive and forget and get on with your life. That is what Jesus would do. B.K. resides on death row in Oklahoma. Sue often writes to him and visits occasionally. She feels that B.K. should never leave prison, but she does not want him executed. She has become friends with B.K. and because of her love and friendship he has become a devout Christian.

Sue states that some good has come out of her Daddy's death."I have been able to witness to many people about Jesus and forgiveness and helped others to heal. I have brought B.K. and many other men on death row to our Lord Jesus Christ. I live in peace with my Lord!" Sue Norton is a member of Murder Victims Families for Reconciliation and the Kansas Coalition to Abolish the Death Penalty. Sue has traveled extensively to speak to schools, churches and community groups about forgiveness and Christianity. Sue gave an eloquent speech to the parole board pleading to save B.K.'s life. Many of the parole board members were in tears but voted for death. B.K. was executed by the state of Oklahoma on May 27, 2003. Bud Welch from Oklahoma City and Aba Gayle from Oregon were both there to support BK and Sue with their loving energy.

RECONCILLIATION

Jo Berry's father was a member of the British Parliament. He was killed by an IRA bomb in 1984. Jo was 27 years old at the time. Jo remembers knowing that she did not want to blame and become bitter. She knew that she wanted to find a way to bring something positive out of the death of her beloved father. Berry tells that she started a journey with no map but with a trust that step-by-step she would find her way. In November 2000 she met Patrick Magee, the man responsible for her father's death. He had been released from prison as part of the Good Friday Peace Agreement.

When Jo looks back on that day, she remembers being scared. Would she regret meeting him? Then the door opened, Patrick arrived and they sat and talked together for three hours. This visit had a sense of intensity that Jo had never felt before. Finally Patrick said, "I have never met anyone like you before. I don't know what to say. I want to hear your pain." Although there were many difficulties, Jo and Patrick continued their meetings and became friends. This made a profound change in both of them. Jo came to realize that if she had lived Patrick's life, she might have done what he did. Patrick came to realize how many innocent victims were created by his violence.

This friendship has been healing for both Jo and Patrick. They now travel the world telling their stories. A play, The Bomb, has been written about them. Jo often does workshops after the play is shown, especially for young people. Jo and Patrick now work together for peace. They speak for The Forgiveness Project. They have spoken in Spain, Austria, South Africa and Palestine/Israel. I hope to bring Jo to the USA to participate in the Journey of Hope.

A BOUQUET FOR MOTHER

A man stopped at a flower shop to order some flowers to be wired to his mother who lived two hundred miles away.

As he got out of his car he noticed a young girl sitting on the curb sobbing.

He asked her what was wrong and she replied, "I wanted to buy a red rose for my mother. But I only have seventy-five cents, and a rose costs two dollars."

The man smiled and said, "Come on in with me. I'll buy you a rose."

He bought the little girl her rose and ordered his own mother's flowers.

As they were leaving he offered the girl a ride home. She said, "Yes, please! You can take me to my mother."

She directed him to a cemetery, where she placed the rose on a freshly dug grave.

The man returned to the flower shop, canceled the wire order, picked up a bouquet and drove the two hundred miles to his mother's house.

ARE YOUR POTATOES HEAVY ?

A teacher once told each of her students to bring a clear plastic bag and a sack of potatoes to school. For every person they refuse to forgive in their life's experience, they chose a potato, wrote on it the name and date, and put it in the plastic bag. Some of their bags were quite heavy. They were then told to carry this bag with them everywhere for one week, putting it beside their bed at night, on the car seat when driving, next to their desk at work. The hassle of lugging this around with them made it clear what a weight they were carrying spiritually, and how they had to pay attention to it all the time to not forget and keep leaving it in embarrassing places. Naturally, the condition of the potatoes deteriorated to a nasty smelly slime. This was a great metaphor for the price we pay for keeping our pain and heavy negativity! Too often we think of forgiveness as a gift to the other person, and it clearly is for ourselves!

THE HIGH ROAD LEADS TO A BIKE

It was a year ago that Joshua Saffle got a bike for Christmas, and he rode it every day. That is, until recently, when the bike was gone from its usual place. Running to his front yard, Joshua, 9, saw a man loading it into his car. He shouted, but the man drove off. Mrs. Saffle said Joshua has strong faith, and told his dad he forgave the thief. What's more, he wanted the thief to know he was forgiven. So the next day, he dictated a message that his mother wrote on a large poster-board. He signed it, stapled it to a sawhorse and put it in the front yard. "To the person who stole my bike: You really hurt my feelings when you took my bike. But I am a Christian and beause (sic) Jesus forgave me, I FORGIVE YOU!!" When Joshua's father left for work the next day, the sign was face-down in the yard. But then, at the end of the driveway, the bike was back, and with new handlebars, grips and a new front fork assembly.

CRUISE DINNERS

This is something I had never experienced, a girl popped up in my face, and I just let her go. A few days back, my family got on a cruise for a holiday. I didn't really like the idea of cruises, but i went anyway. I had a pretty rough year, achieving lower grades in school and not doing so well in my social circle. Being in an all boys school, contacts will members of the opposite sex is very rare. Also, i would consider myself the less sociable kind of guy.

But then at the first dinner night, it happened. I shared a table with my parents and a cousin family. We chose our seats and sat. Then, directly across where i was sitting, about 3 tables away, was a girl, about my age. She carried with her the perfect female face I could ever imagine. From that distance, I could only admire the lager details, but man were they amazing. Her rimmed glasses complemented her eyes, her slightly curled reached just below her shoulders. The face seemed smooth as silk. It really was the image I had long hoped for. Throughout the entire meal, I couldn't stop looking up and admiring her side face features. My appetite was great that night.

The next night came again, and we sat in the exact same seats. Only this time, there was a standing wine Menu slightly blocking my line of sight. Every now and then i would ever so slightly crane my next towards the side to get a glance at her. I guess i was somewhat noticed by my mom, and stopped doing it for a bit. But the feel was still there, and every moment I get to look at her is filled with happiness and curiosity at the same time. By the third day I kind of got a gist of who she is. The girl seemed like an introvert, one that also does not socialise very much.

During the entire duration of the cruise, she always stuck with her parents and her one younger sister. She is the kind of person who takes much care for her siblings. This 'lack of outwardness' is what attracts me. Just a quiet female, also one that seems quite well educated too.

On the last night, I started noticing that she now looks in my direction. Occasionally, she would turn her head to her left, to the direction where I was in, and kind of scans the area before landing her eyes on me, then quickly turning her head back. I was in shock. The past three nights, it was a one way staring contest, but this night, it became two way. We exchange many, many glances throughout the short one hour dinner, but it felt like the one hour of my life at that time. There was this one eye contact that lasted a few seconds, only to be broken by her first. I was in disarray, didn't know what to do. My face carried no smile, no sadness, but it was all in my head and my heart. Finally she took notice of me. I have this gut feeling that she feels somewhat the same too. Come to think of it, I feel embarrassed for re-wearing my shirt on that night :P

I couldn't really go to bed that night. I had this mentality of 'screw everything, just go forth and do it'. The dreams I had were sweet ones, where we met on the topmost sundeck, which is secluded away from the buzz at the pool. Where she was leaning against the railing looking at the sea, and where I approached her. The dream of the first conversation was really nice, but it never happened. The next day was the last day. As suggested in my dreams, I went to the sundeck. No one there. I could feel this emptiness in my heart. I thought the last dinner was the last time I would be able to see her. Sitting on a deckchair for about 30 minutes, then finally deciding to leave. I went to take my breakfast, but every part of my body is telling me that she is still waiting for me on the sundeck. Eventually I made my way up, but focusing more on the scenery this time, knowing that it was all but just a dream after all. Leaning out, looking at the sea. Then, I turned around. She was there right there, in front of my eyes. And her parents. Of course, I did not know what to do, and I definitely wouldn't dare to approach her in front of her parents. So I ran. I ran away from the sundeck. It was a decision that I would regret for the next few nights. I never got to see her again after disembarking. It was both a chanced meeting of joy and sorrow. After thinking, it seems like Fate's work after all. Of all cruise ships, of all the days, of all the restaurants on the vessel, of all the tables, she just had to sit right in front of my eyes. I don't know man. It was the one and only feel I got, one that shocked me into writing this story. Her face, still vivid in my mind. The whole experience was so amazing. In a short span of 5 days I fell for a girl I didn't even know, not even her name. Will I ever meet this beautiful girl again? I guess, I have a feeling Fate is with me.

MY BEST FRIENDS WEDDING

I haven't talked much about this, and that's mostly why I'm doing this. I'm currently in a marriage that will end when my child graduates high school. So, there really isn't anywhere to unload this stuff. I went to my best friend's wedding in Cali. He has a 24yo sister (I'm 38) that took my breath away. From the time I saw her, she was the most beautiful thing I'd ever seen. It was like there was a light beaming from her, screaming at me or slapping me in the face one. I was there a few days, and we never really talked, no get to know you kinda stuff. When i was leaving her presence that final time, I felt something like sorrow. I can recall it now, because I've had time to think about it, but then I didn't really get what was happening. I knew when i was flying away, that something wasn't right, it felt like I was leaving home, instead of going there. I felt like something of me was left behind, but that was really the most discernible feelings i could come up with. I had never felt love before, and I just didn't know it till her.I got home, back to work and life, but for weeks I couldn't focus much, all I had were these feelings that were just roiling inside me, like a massive ball of chaos. I tried to make sense of it, tried to break it down in my mind, figure out if these feeling I had for her were created by me, by my unmet needs, emotional handicaps, falsely created expectations, etc. In the process of this chaos of feeling (which I still didn't get what they were), I messaged her once and asked if she had felt anything for me after I left, and she said no. I thought that might bring closure (although I now know this kind of love is irrepressibly hopeful. There is a part of my heart that always says she is important, no matter how much the evidence says otherwise), but getting her answer changed nothing. I still wrangled over these feeling, and actually fought off the idea of calling it love even though it came to my head many time. Then one day I just realized it was love. Once the chaoses of feeling were over, I found a little peace, but she was planted deeper within. Now it's only certainty of the feeling. I have so many "daydreams" of talking, having all the right things said, etc. It's been 6 months now, and I don't see these feelings subsiding. I think, after a hiatus from the feelings that I'm getting over it, but the next "session" is hits harder and longer. I don't really know how to view it. I don't wanna walk away from it, but I know I can't change it, and am fairly "certain" that it's really not "meant to be". I have thought about telling her how I feel. But I find, when those little daydreams come where we are exactly where I think perfect is, every so often I look into her eyes. I mean, like I feel the stare...and I am ashamed of myself for making her a mistress. I know she deserves better than me, but that doesn't really change my heart. So I go about my days a little emptier, a little darker, and there isn't anything I can do about it. I wish I had never had these feelings, and I feel like it was a great gift. I didn't know at first that what had happened was "love at first site", but I now know it's the closest thing to it I will probably find. I didn't really believe in it at all, except to say I do because a few claim it happened to them. But my experience has left me hurting, not joyful, sad, not happy. I reckon that's life, but at least I got to tell my tale.

IT WAS LATE NIGHT, AT THE BAR OF......

It was late night, at the bar of the camping this summer. He was dancing rock n' roll and then he was standing alone and smoking. It was love at first sight. I knew he was all I ever wanted, my soul mate. I didn't know what to do, but I couldn't help myself, I yelled "hey you!" He yelled "No, no. You don't need to talk to me because I'm standing here alone" (his friends were still dancing), apparently he came closer, he nailed my eyes with his and told me "I'm not an I'm not an interesting person, I'm just not", the truth is I didn't know what to say. So, the first thing that came to my brain was "what kind of music do you like?" and he told me about every single unknown indie, jazz, rock n roll etc. bands I loved.. I thought how is that possible? We had everything in common, EVERYTHING. We left the bar and went for a night swim until morning. He would swim naked. We had the best time of our lives with the most amazing view. I can still hear his voice sometimes. We didn't have sex or anything, we didn't even kiss. But I'm telling you I've had the most amazing telepathic sex ever. We slept together until the evening since I had to leave. It was his first day in the camping; he was A French guy in a Euro trip with friends. We exchanged Facebook accounts, even phone numbers. This was the most short version of the story. It was the best night-day of my life, he changed me inside out it's been 5 months now and my heart still beats for him. I know that love at first sight sounds crazy, but if only if you experience it you will believe there's such a thing one hundred percent. Félix, my everything.

NEVER BELIEVED IN LOVE

Never Believed In Love At First Sight Before It Happened To Me I work as a nurse in a step down unit in a hospital. I'd been single for 6 months and was finally at a place where I accepted it and wasn't trying to turn every first date into marriage. I wasn't looking forward to my schedule that week, Friday, Saturday, and Sunday night but I came to work and started in right away. As I was waiting to get report from the day nurse, I felt as if I was being watched. I looked up and saw him. Tall, dark, and handsome with the most breathtaking smile I've seen. I quickly looked away and felt flushed with embarrassment. There was no way this beautiful man was looking at me. He interrupted me and nonchalantly asked me for a juice. I asked him if the patient was allowed to drink juice and he laughed and said it was for him. I walked to the nutrition room and got him the juice, smiling as I turned away. As soon as he walked away I felt like grabbing him and not letting go, as if I was going to lose him forever. I can still feel the emotions inside of me that I felt at that moment. I came to work the next day and there he was. Leaning against the wall by the nurse's station. with that same smile. He tried to hold my gaze but my embarrassment quickly took over again and I tried with everything in my power to not glance his way. I finished up with report and walked into my first patient's room. There he was, sitting on a chair, at the bedside of my patient. I could not believe that out of all the rooms on my floor, I ended up being assigned to that one. I introduced myself as the nurse and the rest was history. My patient was his boss, he had come to visit him and the first thing his boss said to me was "I'm trying to find him a wife!" The next few hours were spent laughing and conversing with my patient and him. He asked me for my number before he left and I don't think I could have given it to him any faster. The next day he visited his boss again, and stayed even longer.

On our first date, I remember walking up behind him sitting on the patio of the restaurant as he held flowers for me. That was the best first date I've had. We are getting married in August. He is an amazing man and I cannot wait to be married to him. I always believed love at first sight was for fools until I experienced it myself. Writing this has incited all the beautiful emotions I felt for him the first time I laid eyes on him. Those feelings still resonate today, with even greater intensity. Don't give up on love.

LIGHTNING STRIKE AT THE AIRPORT

I experienced love at first sight. It was January 9th 2008 at Aberdeen Airport and I remember it like it was yesterday. I was being sent to Stavanger, Norway, with work and was at the airport. I was nervous because I had never met any of the people I was to be working with for the next month. My flight flashed up on the screen as 'Go to Gate 12' and I made my way there. It was sometime before we were due to begin boarding so I sat down and waited, watching the other people on my flight arrive. That's when I saw him; he was walking towards my departure lounge. I never realised why there was the clichéd phrase, 'It was like being hit by lightning,' until I felt it - it really is like being hit by lightning. All of a sudden my heart was racing, I had butterflies in my tummy, and my hands were sweating.

He sat down in the seat opposite me. I didn't say anything and barely made eye contact with him. I'd been hurt a lot in the past, I'm shy and I also couldn't see the point in striking up a conversation with someone I'd never see again. I spent the time glancing over at him and was embarrassed to find myself making eye contact with him repeatedly but also quite pleased that he was obviously looking over at me a lot too. I couldn't help but admire him - he was gorgeous.

Our plane was called for departure. He got up shortly after I did and was a few people behind me in the queue. As we headed for our seats, the people separating us sat down in there's until he was behind me. I wasn't looking at him but I was aware of everything he was doing (or more to the point, hyper-aware). I came to my seat, put my bag in the overhead locker, and looked straight into his eyes. My heart stopped beating. I hated feeling so out of control and broke eye contact and never returned his beautiful smile. I spent the rest of the hour-long flight listening to his conversation with the girl next to him - he was in the seat right behind mine.

On the way off the plane, I tried to get through quickly. I didn't know anyone who I was meant to be working with, where I was meant to meet them and didn't want to get left behind at the airport. I stopped at the bathroom and then went straight to the baggage halls. My bag, complete with the company name and logo, was the only one left (so much for being quick) and my gorgeous man was there waiting for me. And that's when I realised that he was one of my new colleagues. He introduced himself to me. And that's when I realised I was a goner. Never in my life, and certainly not after the trauma my ex-boyfriends have put me through, had I met someone, a complete stranger that I instantly trusted. This man was different. I would have put my life in his hands at that very moment. My heart was beating out of control and I wouldn't be surprised if my pupils were dilated.

That was almost two years ago and we're still together. I still get butterflies in my stomach, a wildly beating heart and sweaty hands when I see him. No-one ever believes the story of how we met, particularly not the lightning strikes, but I think some people just never get to experience love at first sight. I feel lucky that I did. Being apart from him for even a few hours is painful. I wonder if I experienced a double whammy - love at first sight with my soul mate.

HOPELESSLY IN LOVE WITH THE PERSON

Hopelessly In Love With The Person Who Doesn't Want To See Me I can't believe that I am writing something about my life, which I never did. The only reason I lost her because what of what I'm doing right now. Sharing my thoughts with others thinking that it would help me and my feeling about her. Her name is Tanisha.

I met her in this summer in my school when I was hanging out with some of my lady friends. That time when I saw her I had two baseball tickets with me and seeing her I couldn't think anything but finding a pen to write my phone number on the baseball ticket and hand it to her. She actually took it and then we start sending msg through facebook and I asked her saying," why don't you let me draw your cute face and I actually did it. So I sent it to her through facebook. She kept on sending me msg too but in a way that would believe that she is not into me. That summer she was with someone and then next time when I saw her, which was the beginning of our fall semester.

Every time when I see her I wanted to make at least a min of conversation. I have to say I was acting with her like I was a big flirt. I guess I have to mention something else that I was that type guy who would hit on any girl who would pass by me. Am not an attractive but a decent guy and used to hang out girls all the time. I didn't take her seriously that time. Then one day I saw her again in the library with her fiends that she hangs out all the time. She is that type girl who takes words from her friends.

So I saw her in the library and after talking to them for couple min I left. As soon I stepped outside I had a text message from an unknown number saying "hey, you look cute today, want to go out watch movie sometime." As I was a big flirt I replied saying," hey I like the fact you use the same thing that I do too, which is ask someone out to dinner random, but can I at least see you or have a firm hand shake?" then we kept texting each other didn't know who it was. One day that number texted me saying," hey I'm prego so I don't go to school, can you be my babies daddy? "and replied saying,' I don't think I will be able to afford to be anyone's daddy now." But if it is a daughter then I would have to consider something else, I guess."

I know this is weird saying that last text reply, but the only reason I did it cos I found out that it was Tanisha by calling that number using my friend's phone number. So after that she found out that I knew that it was me and then she stop texting me. But I made a plan just to reveal that it was Tanisha that I was talking to her. And then she actually revealed herself by saying," OMG it's my friends who used my phone and texted you all these, I didn't know any of these. I didn't believe her that time. Thought that she likes me a bit. And then we start texting each other like regular friends.

I sketched one of her pictures form facebook that I was obsessed with. So I did it on the back of my Resume and gave it to her. She Liked that Drawing. I was happy that she liked it. Somehow I felt something about her. Her friends start to asking me, "hey so are you and Tanisha are getting along? Are you guys like doing something? "And I start to think about her. I think I did like her than any other girls in my life. Then one day I was eating bagel in the café and I saw her and as soon I approached her I kept on munching the bagel and she told me that she is getting engaged. First I thought that she was kidding. Then after couple weeks I start hearing that she is actually getting engaged with the guy chosen by her parents. But I didn't believe it. I thought she is doing it cos she didn't want me she her.

I don't know why knowing that she doesn't want me or she doesn't like me that way I still believed that may be a lil bit of her that has something for me.

Which is when I wrote a poem how I felt about her. It was snowing and it looked so beautiful outside and I felt like if she was with me right now and send her the poem. This is the first time I told her about my feelings, but by texting. then she texted me saying," I'm so cheesy" and I said," cos you I am like this now" then we stop texting for a week and then I saw one of her friends. I told her what I did and she said," dude why would you do this, this is creepy; you don't know her that way. She prolly creped out" I thought she prolly did.

One night I made up my mind that I will tell her the truth that how I feel about her. And this time I will tell her in person. not by texting. Next day when I saw her something unusual happened to me that never happened in my life. I couldn't say a word to her but just waved my hand saying hi. I tried so hard to talk to her. But couldn't. I couldn't sleep the whole night. I realized that this is the first time I am emotionally getting attached with someone in my life. Also realized how special she is. The next day she texted me after 3 weeks saying," hey how do you know this girl name Lora? I've seen pic with you and her." I said," Before you say anything I wanted to tell you something." She replied," it's too late for you to say anything. "I couldn't understand her respond. Then I said," I am sorry, I might creped you out by that poem." She said," how do you know that I creped out, if you want to say something then why you couldn't say it to me but believing others. You should talk to me direct. You know? You are man. You should know."

I realized that she wanted me to talk to her personally. And I did, next day I went to school keeping that in mind that no matter how hard it is to tell her that I like her and ask her out nicely. Even though I knew that I would mess it up, cos I was nervous. So she was with her friends and I told her, " you want to walk outside for a min, I want to tell you something."

We went up for a walk. It was the coldest evening in my life. I was shivering the whole time when she was walking with me. Then It happen, I told her, she said, "look I knew for a long time that you do like me, I was giving you points, I took some points though, cos you were eating bagels in front me. "

Then I asked her out. That was the first time I've seen her real herself. I knew that she was being herself. I realized she doesn't be herself when she is with her friends. Then she said, "Look if we go out then I don't want to let my friends know. Cos they spread the rumors to the whole school. "So didn't know that did she say yes or no. she was being mad confusing. After that I got on the bus with her and somehow she mentioned something about buying a jacket and I told her why she doesn't let me buy her the jacket. (I bought this jacket and don't know how to tell her that i did). She goes like," hey now I've lil pimples on my face why do you even like me. "I said," that really doesn't affect the way I like you, even if you were crippled which I hope you won't I will still want to be with you." then we were about to get on the train and I said, "I want to see you tomorrow." She said," If you want to see me then you would have to get off from the train." Cos I was going to drop her home. So again the whole night I couldn't sleep and I went to school and tried to talk to one of her close friends. As I didn't get any answer either it's yes or no I assumed that even though she is not into me or doesn't want to go out cos she just got outta relationship, may be there's still a chance. May be her friends could help me. Then I talked to one of her friends and I told her everything about the lil walk and the conversation between me and Tanihsa on that evening.

That was my biggest mistake. Her friend spread the rumor to everyone in the school and now she knows it too. So she got upset and she texted me saying," what is wrong with you. Why can't you not shut your mouth? Why you spreading rumor to everyone when nothing happened between us, FOR A SECOND I THOUGHT YOU ARE A NICE GUY. YOU RUINED EVERYTHING. do not talk to me or tried to come near me. Get it right or I will restrain an order against you. "I told her everything that I didn't say everything to everyone and she couldn't believe me. She said, "Stop lying to me." Then I replied, "fine I wasn't gonna see you again anyway."

I LIED TO HER. I CANT THINK ANYTHING STRAIGHT NOW. I CAN'T EVEN EAT. THAT NIGHT I TRIED TO FORGET ABOUT HER BUT I

COULDN'T. I SMOKED TOO MUCH AND SPEND TO WHOLE NIGHT OUT SIDE OF THE ROOF WHEN IT WAS 29F. I TALKED TO ONE OF HER GUY FRIENDS AND ASKED HIM," HEY MAN DID SHE EVER MENTION ME?" HE SAID," SHE DID. SHE USED TO SAY NO, I DON'T THINK IF WE GET TOGETHER IT WOULDN'T WORK OUT. MAY BE SHE IS AFRAID OF GOING BACK OUT HERE.

Everything I do I think of her. Everyone I see I see her. I even tried to talk to DR. Mallet who is working on inventing the TIME MACHINE thinking that IF I COULD BACK TO PAST AND NOT

TALK TO HER FRIENDS WHO messed ME UP. I WISH I COULD MAKE HER BELIEVE HOW MUCH I LIKE NO I ACTUALLY LOVE HER. IT SUCKS NOT SAYING SOMEONE YOU LOVE BUT THAT YOU LOVE HER. I don't know what would take to get her back even though I never had her. But I could have had her. COS SHE SAID I RUINED EVERYTHING AND HER GUY FRIENDS COMMENTS makes me thinking that I could've change something.

I Love you Tani Sahid. I would do anything to get you back. I know I'm a mess and I believe you could fix me. The more I try not to think about you the more you come to my dream. Not even being with me, you are with me, the whole day, the whole minute, every time that I wanted to break to change the past.

INSTANT CONNECTION

At First Sight - Happened To Me Twice I don't believe in actual love at first sight - love takes time to develop. But twice in my life when I was young,(I'm now 48) I have met guys that I felt an instant and inexplicable connection to. The first time was in 1979, I was only 14 and he was all of 13. Babies, really. This was in Jr. high and I was grade 10, and he was grade 8. I will call him "Sam".

I saw him walking down the hall and thought to myself " that guy is pretty cute for a grade 8", and as he walked past I happened to look straight into his eyes. Now here is the really weird part: as our eyes met I seemed to "hear a voice in my head". That's how I can only explain it. And no, I don't normally hear voices! Anyway, the voice said something like this "You've just seen the guy you might end up marrying one day". As you might imagine, I was shocked and amazed.

Anyways, as things turned out, this guy became a friend of my younger sister's boyfriend, so I would run into him here and there. I didn't have a crush on him at that point, but I did feel a really weird feeling when I was around him. He made me nervous - but actually I didn't like him all that much thought he was kind of annoying and arrogant.

Now a few years later, when we were 19 and 20, I started to feel differently. However, he didn't seem to have any interest in me at all - so I didn't pursue the matter. Sorry for the long story, but bear with me here, there is a point to all this.....just takes a while to get to it!

So right around this time I started a new job. One of the first days on the job, I am sitting in the staff room, and one of the employees I hadn't met yet walked in. I will call him Tom. I looked up at him and everything just stopped. Like a sappy romantic movie or something - everything else just faded away.

He was staring directly at me and my only thought was "Is it possible that gorgeous guy is looking at me!!" Apparently he was, as I heard his friend say to him "quit staring at the girl - what's the matter do you want to marry her or something?"

Now if you're thinking we ran into each other arms or something equally romantic - nope, that didn't happen. Seems like we could never really let each other know how we felt, though we did become friends over time. As it was I started going out with another guy that worked there - one of his friends. That turned out to be a mistake. Then Tom set me up with another of his friends and I started going out with him, and Tom started going out with another girl who also worked there. Often a whole group of us would hang out together. I started feeling more and more drawn to Tom.

After a while Tom broke up with this girl. One night we were hanging out, having a few too many drinks, my boyfriend left the room. Tom was sitting beside me and decided to put his head on my lap, and for some reason I decided to kiss him. Just a small kiss, but it soon turned very passionate. The next thing I know is I hear my boyfriend yelling, and one of his other friends, who were also there, noticed what, was going on between us and actually pulled Tom away from me. I believe he thought he was hurting me - which wasn't the case at all. We just seemed to lose all control.

So, of course, the boyfriend is yelling, I'm feeling totally confused, and I'm not proud of this, but I ended up making a terrible decision. I didn't want the guys to fight; Tom was looking at me with such intense eyes, boyfriend yelling "do you want to be with him instead?" I'm thinking of all the gossip that going to be spread about me at work, and I did the wrong thing. I should have followed my heart, and threw myself into Tom's arms, regardless of what would happen, because you can't ever know if something will work if you don't give it a try. And regrettably I didn't give it a try.

So after this, there was too much hurt to go back. The damage was done, and couldn't be repaired. The boyfriend broke up with me a few weeks later - he knew I was really in love with Tom and couldn't admit it. Anyways, my heart was broken, especially since I knew I was the one who screwed the whole thing up. Now this brings us back to the first guy, Sam. Several months later, I showed up a party, wearing a sexy Halloween costume, and all of a sudden he was totally interested. Seems all it took was a sexy costume.......if only I'd known earlier! We have been together over 25 years now - not perfect, but a good marriage. I have asked him if he noticed me all those years ago, and he claims not to have. I guess it was a one-sided attraction on my part. I have no idea why I had the sudden thought I would one day marry him, but sometimes truth is stranger than fiction I guess. I still think of Tom and wonder what would have happened if I made a different decision that night. Would all our lives be different now? Kinda makes me want to get into that "back to the future" Deloreon and find out.

THE LADY WITH THE BEAUTIFUL SMILE

I work in the main building of the Scottish Government in Edinburgh. There was a lady who used to work on the second floor as a boss, and she was really attractive. We used to see each other in the passing, and we both would say hi and exchange a smile between us. One time she came through the door on her way to the car and she just blew me away, i just melted and said WOW. She had short black hair and was wearing a lovely dress; she carried herself well and was highly educated. She looked across at me for a brief moment and the eye contact was something else, don't know how to explain this to others, you know when something transpires between two people-and there is an understanding of a sort? I only seen her briefly after that before she left, and again the beautiful smile and eye contact was still there. Strangely enough i found myself having sleepless nights thinking about her and wondered if it could have been my imagination working overtime or something, but on reflection i think she felt the same. All i can say is that Miss NB blew me away....and if i never see her again i will always remember that beautiful smile and the eye contact we shared. She was something special.

APPOINTMENT BY FATE

I always heard stories about love at first sight. Well, mine was pretty bizarre and it almost like as if it was from a book or a movie. First I want to mention was I am born deaf and I have cochlear implants. One on my left was recent one and my right side was old one. My story takes place at my audiologist appointment. I am Christian and

I believed it was God's plan for us to meet, but if you are non-believer, called it fate. I believe it was part of God's plan because this guy was answer to my prayers. I prayed to God that I wish someone who can understand me on what I went through. Then prayer later, I prayed to God that I felt like there is going to be somebody will come along and I want to be prepared. This happens in one week before my appointment. * means names change.

At audiologist office, I was in sound booth for testing on both ears with two implants. I heard my mom and my audiologist were talking. I was frustrated with my left side because I can't hear as well as my right side. Then, I realized my right side was also not doing well. I cried so hard. My mom came in and soothe me. My mom then said, "Your audiologist, Nancy* was telling me about this guy who is close to your age who went through exact same thing." Nancy said, "His name is Taylor*. You both are motivated and intelligent students and very close to same age. He has his recently. I feel like you two have same struggles." I am like okay. Then, I felt little better. Nancy led me to a room.

Then, I saw Taylor for the first time. I am like oh my gosh. It was unbelievable feelings. Then, I watch him tripped all over a cord because he was also on an appointment. I giggled and I said, "It happens all the time". Well it's true. Then we shook our hands. On the outside, I look calm and introduced myself. On the inside, I am like feeling completely swoon or heart pounding. I feel like I met him before. Another odd part of this story was I dream about him before long before I met him. Very odd.

We only met for less than a minute. Nancy said that we should exchange emails. Nancy moved me to another room. Later, Taylor gave me his email. Then, I gave mine. Then, next day, we emailed to each other in at least 14 messages. Our emails described to be personal life experiences and flirty.

He compliment on my outfit on what I had on my appointment. I thought I had on my worse outfit ever. I had on light washed jeans and my oversize sweatshirt. We still email to each other. More I talk to him; the more I realized how much we have in common and similar beliefs. We only know each other for a month to this day, so I don't know if we will ever be boyfriend/girlfriend or possible marriage. I keep getting a feeling that he might be the one. The coolest part of the story was Nancy was talking to Taylor and he was expressing his frustration, then she thought of me. And coincidentally, I was coming in for an appointment on that very day. My mom told me that Nancy had said that she does not normally play matchmaker, but....they need each other. Is it that funny? We have been match by our audiologist. We have a lot of coincidence experiences in our life. For example, his birthday was exact same date as when I had my surgery on my cochlear implant. We both had exact same bad years. Taylor trusted me enough to share his insecurity stories. Do you want to know how I came up name "Taylor" for this guy? His hotness level is like Taylor Lautner and he likes wolves because of New Moon. How funny is that. Maybe we might end up together. I don't know. I hope so. We will see. I thank God so many times for him.

HAPPY AND SAD AT THE SAME

Happy And Sad At The Same Time! There's this person in my life...known them about 2 years. I have never communicated so much through my eyes with any person in my life. i now truly understand the expression, "eyes are the windows to the soul." when i look into their eyes, i can just see all of their thoughts, feelings, hopes, fears, worries...just everything - including how they feel about me. I think we both have an on/off switch on our eyes. When others are around and we don't want to reveal our feelings, we can pull a shade over our eyes and they become vacant. But sometimes, we lift the shades and BOOM. When we look into each other's eyes, it takes my breath away. My heart stops, Lightning strikes me, every time. I quickly try to diffuse the electricity and look away or say something mundane because if i don't, i swear i will get completely electrocuted. I am just too weak to handle more than a few seconds of looking into those eyes. The first time i met them, the first thing that occurred to me was, and "where have you been all my life?" it was like relief just swept over me, like "there you are. I finally found you and now my life is complete." i felt like i had known them my whole life. We are so, so different but eerily similar in certain ways. We are intellectually, spiritually, emotionally, psychologically and physically aligned. The way we process things, the way we think, our sense of humor, our egos, our tempers, our interests and hobbies. We speak our own dialect - the way we use words and put sentences together is identical. We can say half a sentence and trail off because there is no point in wasting energy saying what the other knows. It's almost as if we have telepathy. Yet, we couldn't be more different in terms of race, religion, ethnicity, family background, age, life experiences, you name it. It's literally like 2 duplicate souls were planted into 2 completely different, random people in the world. But somehow, their paths crossed. It's just bizarre. I feel so understood by this person. They somehow understood me from day 1 and they understand me better than my own family or my closest friends do. What i have always thought of as my faults and that my family always criticized me for, this person somehow values and embraces. It's almost as if this person's acceptance of me is slowly healing deep wounds in my heart. I feel that i am doing the same for them in a way. We are both a little messed in the head in certain subtle ways that only the other person understands and can cure. This relationship is full of so much good for both of us. It's helping us improve and evolve in so many ways. I am so blessed for the gift of this person in my life. Sadly, we are both in relationships so nothing will ever come out of this. It's purely platonic. We have to interact regularly, but we keep a permanent barrier between us. Sometimes you meet that special, rare person but the circumstances are such that you can't be together. "Star-crossed" is the appropriate expression. I suppose it's a test from God. Can you endure a life without them (not entirely without them, but with them only from a distance) for the sake of taking the higher moral ground? Even though you have to undergo daily torture. Some days aren't too bad - you get busy and time goes by quickly. But other days are...agonizing.

It's not that i don't love my significant other either. I love them very, very deeply. They are two very different types of loves that serve very different purposes. Just the way love for a child is different, or love for a friend is different. I wish i could tell this person that i love them. I wish i could say the words to them. I know it won't change anything, and in fact it's probably a very, very bad idea considering our situation. But maybe they will read this. And, like always, with that weird 6th sense we seem to have with each other, will sense it's coming from me and just feel happy knowing that there is someone out there in the world that completely understands, loves and accepts them. So, my special someone, if you are reading this - I love you. All of you, for all time, in every form, no matter what we face. If you were to ever tell me you love me too, i will be too weak to resist you, so i beg you never to say it either. This will be a secret whispered between our two hearts and that's where it will stay.

THE GIRL AT BUS STOP

I saw this girl almost every day while coming from the office. We saw each other.. Exchange our glance... and go away in our path. The best thing or worst that i am developing a big crush on her day by day... i m helpless. I just have that 15 to 20 seconds or maximum 30 seconds that I spend with her...but believe me i am waiting that moment every day. I don't have a clue what is happening. The day when i do not see her. It is like something is missing on that day...God...her small eyes. Shoulder length hair. Her looks. Really driving me crazy. Everyday i think i will approach her but the very moment i can't. I don't know what i should do but the feeling is just nostalgic

WHO OR WHAT DO WE LOVE MORE?

A man was polishing his new car; his 4 yr old daughter picked up a stone and scratched on the side of the car. In anger, the furious Man took his child's hand & hit it many times, not realizing he was using a wrench. At the hospital, the child lost all his fingers due to multiple fractures. When the child saw her father, with painful eyes he asked 'Dad when will my fingers grow back?' The man was so hurt and speechless. He went back to the car and kicked it many times. Devastated by his own actions, sitting in front of the car he looked at the scratches, His daughter had written 'LOVE YOU DAD'.

Moral: Remember, Anger and Love have no limit. Always remember that "Things are to be used and people are to be loved". But the problem in today's world is that "People are being used & Things are being loved".

A BOUQUET FOR MOTHER

A man stopped at a flower shop to order some flowers to be wired to his mother who lived two hundred miles away. As he got out of his car he noticed a young girl sitting on the curb sobbing. He asked her what was wrong and she replied, "I wanted to buy a red rose for my mother. But I only have seventy-five cents, and a rose costs two dollars."

The man smiled and said, "Come on in with me. I'll buy you a rose."

He bought the little girl her rose and ordered his own mother's flowers.

As they were leaving he offered the girl a ride home. She said, "Yes, please! You can take me to my mother. "She directed him to a cemetery, where she placed the rose on a freshly dug grave. The man returned to the flower shop, canceled the wire order, picked up a bouquet and drove the two hundred miles to his mother's house.

FULFILLING A PROMISE

Ever since the beginning, the girl's family member disagree her relationship with the boy. Saying that because of family background, if she insists of being together with the boy, she'll suffer for her whole lifetime. Because of the pressure applied by family members, she frequently quarrels with him. The girl does love the boy; she used to ask him, "How much do you love me?" Because the boy is not good with words, he used to make her angry. With additional comment from her parents, her moods get even worse. The boy has become her "anger releasing target". And the boy, just silently allowed her to continuously release her anger on him.

Later, the boy graduated from University. He plan to further study overseas but before he left. He proposed to the girl… " I, don't know how to say nice words but I do know that, I love you. If you agree, I am willing to take care of you, the whole life. About your family members, I will work hard to convince them and agree on us."

"Marry me, will you?" the girl agreed.

And her parents, looking at the effort shown by the boy, agreed with them. Finally, before the boy go oversea, they are engaged. The girl stay back in the hometown, step into the working society where as the boy continuing his study oversea. They maintained their relationship through telephone and letters.

Although time is difficult to get through with, but both of them never give up.

One day, the girl left home for work as usual on her way to the bus stop, a car lose control and knock her down. As she awake from unconsciousness, she saw her parents and realize how seriously she got hurt and how fortunate of her, not to get killed.

Looking at her parents, with their faced got all wet by their tears, she tried to comfort them. But then, she found out that She can't even spell out a word, she tried her best to make some voice but all she managed, was to breathe without any voice. She's mute. According to the doctor, the injury affected her brain, and that cause her to be mute for the rest of her life. Listening to her parents persuade, but can't even reply with a single word, the girl collapsed. Throughout the days, others than crying silently, still it is crying.

Later, the girl discharged from hospital. Returning to her home, everything is still like before. Except that the phone ring, has turned into the worst nightmare of hers. Ring after ring, continuously stimulate her, stimulating her pain But she can't tell the boy. She don't want to be a burden to him, and wrote him a letter telling him that she no longer want to wait, the relationship between them ended, and even returned him the engagement ring. Facing the letters and telephone from the boy, all she can do, is to allow tears falling from her eyes.

Her father decided to move, after seeing the pain she is suffering. Hoping that she could forget everything and be happier into a new environment, the girl started to learn, slowly picking up sign language and start over again. Also telling herself to forget the boy.

One day, her best friend tell her that the boy's back. He's searching all around for her, she asked her best friend not to tell him about her and asked her to tell him to forget her. After that for more than a year there was no news of boy. One day her best friend tells her, that the boy is getting married soon, and passed the Wedding Card to her. She open the card sadly, but she found her name on the card.

The moment she want to ask her best friend,

the boy appear in front of her. With an unfamiliar sign language, he told her "I spent more than a year's time, to force myself to learn sign language, in order to tell you, I have not forgot our promise, give me an opportunity, let me be your voice. I love you."

Looking at the slow sign language by the boy, and the engagement ring she gave back to him, she finally smiled.

Moral: Do not be a coward and run away whenever there is a problem, remember that every problem has a solution, never ever break someone's heart; you may not know when it will happen to you.

STORY OF REGRET

There was this guy who believed very much in true love and decided to take his time to wait for his right girl to appear. He believed that there would definitely be someone special out there for him, but none came. Every year at Christmas, his ex-girlfriend would return from Vancouver to look him up. He was aware that she still held some hope of re-kindling the past romance with him. He did not wish to mislead her in any way. So he would always get one of his girl friends to pose as his steady whenever she came back.

That went on for several years and each year; the guy would get a different girl to pose as his romantic interest.

So whenever the ex-girlfriend came to visit him, she would be led into believing that it was all over between her and the guy. The girl took all those rather well, often trying to casually tease him about his different girlfriends, or so, as it seemed! In fact, the girl often wept in secret whenever she saw him with another girl, but she was too proud to admit it. Still, every Christmas, she returned, hoping to re-kindle some form of romance. But each time, she returned to Vancouver feeling disappointed.

Finally she decided that she could not play that game any longer. Therefore, she confronted him and professed that after all those years, he was still the only man that she had ever loved. Although the guy knew of her feelings for him, he was still taken back and have never expected her to react that way. He always thought that she would slowly forget about him over time and come to terms that it was all over between them. Although he was touched by her undying love for him and wanted so much to accept her again, he remembered why he rejected her in the first place-she was not the one he wanted. So he hardened his heart and turned her down cruelly. Since then, three years have passed and the girl never return anymore. They never even wrote to each other. The guy went on with his life… still searching for the one but somehow deep inside him, he missed the girl.

On the Christmas of 1995, he went to his friend's party alone. "Hey, how come all alone this year? Where are all your girlfriends? What happened to that Vancouver babe who joins you every Christmas?" asked one of his friends. He felt warm and comforted by his friend's queries about her, still he just surged on.

Then, he came upon one of his many girlfriends whom he once requested to pose as his steady. He wanted so much to ignore her ….. Not that he was impolite, but because at that moment, he just didn't feel comfortable with those girlfriends anymore. It was almost like he was being judged by them. The girl saw him and shouted across the floor for him. Unable to avoid her, he went up to acknowledge her.

"Hi… how are you? Enjoying the party?" the girl asked.

"Sure… yeah!" he replied.

She was slightly tipsy… must be from the whiskey on her hand. She continued, "Why…? Don't you need someone to pose as your girlfriend this year?" Then he answered, "No, there is no need for that anymore…"

Before he can continue, he was interrupted, "Oh yes! Must have found a girlfriend! You haven't been searching for one for the past years, right?" The man looked up, as if he has struck gold, his face beamed and looked directly at the drunken girl. He replied, "Yes… you are right! I haven't been looking for anyone for the past years."

With that, the man darted across the floor and out the door, leaving the lady in much bewilderment. He finally realized that he has already found his dream girl, and she was… the Vancouver girl all along! The drunken lady has said something that awoken him.

All along he has found his girl. That was why he did not bother to look further when he realized she was not coming back. It was not any specific girl he was seeking! It was perfection that he wanted, and yes… perfection! Relationship is something both parties should work on. Realizing that he had let away someone so important in his life, he decided to call her immediately. His whole mind was flooded with fear. He was afraid that she might have found someone new or no longer had the same feelings anymore… For once, he felt the fear of losing someone.

As it was Christmas Eve, the line was quite hard to get through, especially an overseas call. He tried again and again, never giving up. Finally, he got through…. precisely at 1200 midnight. He confessed his love for her and the girl was moved to tears. It seemed that she never got over him! Even after so long, she was still waiting for him, never giving up.

He was so excited to meet her and to begin his new chapter of their lives. He decided to fly to Vancouver to join her. It was the happiest time of their lives! But their happy time was short-lived. Two days before he was supposed to fly to Vancouver, he received a call from her father. She had a head-on car collision with a drunken driver. She passed away after 6 hours in a coma.

The guy was devastated, as it was a complete loss. Why did fate played such cruel games with him? He cursed the heaven for taking her away from him, denying even one last look at her! How cruel he cursed! How he damned the Gods…!! How he hated himself… for taking so long to realize his mistake!! That was in 1996.

Moral: Treasure what you have… Time is too slow for those who wait, Too swift for those who fear, Too long for those who grief, Too short for those who rejoice, But for those who love… Time is Eternity. For all you out there with someone special in your heart, cherish that person, cherish every moment that you spend together that special someone, for in life, anything can happen anytime. You may painfully regret, only to realize that it is too late.

WHY SHOULD I FEEL BAD?

Once, there was this guy, who was in love with a girl. She wasn't the most beautiful and gorgeous but for him, she was everything. He used to dream about her, about spending the rest of life with her. His friends told him, "why do you dream so much about her, when you don't even know if she loves you or not? First tell her your feelings, and get to know if she likes you or not". He felt that was the right way. The girl knew from the beginning, that this guy loves her. One day when he proposed, she rejected him. His friends thought he would take alcohol; drugs etc. and ruin his life. To their surprise, he was not depressed.When they asked him how was it that he is not sad, he replied, ""why should I feel bad? I lost one who never loved me and she lost the one who really loved and cared for her." Moral: True Love is Hard to Get. Love is all about giving to other person without greed of gaining anything in return, if other person rejects it, it's him/her who will be losing the most important thing in life.

So never feel dejected.

UNTIL DEATH DO US APART

When I got home that night as my wife served dinner, I held her hand and said, I've got something to tell you. She sat down and ate quietly. Again I observed the hurt in her eyes. Suddenly I didn't know how to open my mouth. But I had to let her know what I was thinking. I want a divorce. I raised the topic calmly. She didn't seem to be annoyed by my words, instead she asked me softly, why? I avoided her question. This made her angry. She threw away the chopsticks and shouted at me, you are not a man! That night, we didn't talk to each other. She was weeping. I knew she wanted to find out what had happened to our marriage. But I could hardly give her a satisfactory answer; she had lost my heart to Jane. I didn't love her anymore. I just pitied her! With a deep sense of guilt, I drafted a divorce agreement which stated that she could own our house, our car, and 30% stake of my company. She glanced at it and then tore it into pieces. The woman who had spent ten years of her life with me had become a stranger. I felt sorry for her wasted time, resources and energy but I could not take back what I had said for I loved Jane so dearly. Finally she cried loudly in front of me, which was what I had expected to see. To me her cry was actually a kind of release. The idea of divorce which had obsessed me for several weeks seemed to be firmer and clearer now. The next day, I came back home very late and found her writing something at the table. I didn't have supper but went straight to sleep and fell asleep very fast because I was tired after an eventful day with Jane. When I woke up, she was still there at the table writing. I just did not care so I turned over and was asleep again.

In the morning she presented her divorce conditions. She didn't want anything from me, but needed a month's notice before the divorce. She requested that in that one month, we both try to live as normal a life as possible. Her reason for this conditions were simple. Our son had his exams in a month's time and she didn't want to disrupt him with our broken marriage.

This was agreeable to me. But she had something more, she asked me to recall how I had carried her into out bridal room on our wedding day. She requested that every day for the month's duration I carry her out of our bedroom to the front door ever morning. I thought she was going crazy. Just to make our last days together bearable I accepted her odd request.

I told Jane about my wife's divorce conditions. She laughed loudly and thought it was absurd. No matter what tricks she applies, she has to face the divorce, she said scornfully.

My wife and I hadn't had any body contact

since my divorce intention was explicitly expressed. So when I carried her out on the first day, we both appeared clumsy. Our son clapped behind us, daddy is holding mommy in his arms. His words brought me a sense of pain. From the bedroom to the sitting room, then to the door, I walked over ten meters with her in my arms. She closed her eyes and said softly; don't tell our son about the divorce. I nodded, feeling somewhat upset. I put her down outside the door. She went to wait for the bus to work. I drove alone to the office.

On the second day, both of us acted much more easily. She leaned on my chest. I could smell the fragrance of her blouse. I realized that I hadn't looked at this woman carefully for a long time. I realized she was not young any more. There were fine wrinkles on her face, her hair was graying! Our marriage had taken its toll on her. For a minute I wondered what I had done to her.

On the fourth day, when I lifted her up, I felt a sense of intimacy returning. This was the woman who had given ten years of her life to me. On the fifth and sixth day, I realized that our sense of intimacy was growing again. I didn't tell Jane about this. It became easier to carry her as the month slipped by. Perhaps the everyday workout made me stronger.

She was choosing what to wear one morning. She tried on quite a few dresses but could not find a suitable one. Then she sighed, all my dresses have grown bigger. I suddenly realized that she had grown so thin, that was the reason why I could carry her more easily. Suddenly it hit me. She had buried so much pain and bitterness in her heart. Subconsciously I reached out and touched her head.

Our son came in at the moment and said, Dad, it's time to carry mom out. To him, seeing his father carrying his mother out had become an essential part of his life. My wife gestured to our son to come closer and hugged him tightly. I turned my face away because I was afraid I might change my mind at this last-minute. I then held her in my arms, walking from the bedroom, through the sitting room, to the hallway. Her hand surrounded my neck softly and naturally. I held her body tightly; it was just like our wedding day.

But her much lighter weight made me sad. On the last day, when I held her in my arms I could hardly move a step. Our son had gone to school. I held her tightly and said, I hadn't noticed that our life lacked intimacy. I drove to office and jumped out of the car swiftly without locking the door. I was afraid any delay would make me change my mind. I walked upstairs. Jane opened the door and I said to her, Sorry, Jane, I do not want the divorce anymore.

She looked at me, astonished, and then touched my forehead. Do you have a fever? She said. I moved her hand off my head.

Sorry, Jane, I said, I won't divorce. My marriage life was boring probably because she and I didn't value the details of our lives, not because we didn't love each other anymore. Now I realize that since I carried her into my home on our wedding day I am supposed to hold her until death do us apart. Jane seemed to suddenly wake up. She gave me a loud slap and then slammed the door and burst into tears. I walked downstairs and drove away. At the floral shop on the way, I ordered a bouquet of flowers for my wife. The sales girl asked me what to write on the card. I smiled and wrote, "I'll carry you out every morning until death do us apart".

That evening I arrived home, flowers in my hands, a smile on my face, I run up stairs, only to find my wife in the bed – dead.

My wife had been fighting cancer for months and I was so busy with Jane to even notice. She knew that she would die soon and she wanted to save me from the negative reaction from our son, in case we push through with the divorce. At least, in the eyes of our son— I'm a loving husband.

Moral: The small details of your lives are what really matter in a relationship. It is not the mansion, the car, property, the money in the bank. These create an environment conducive for happiness but cannot give happiness in themselves. So find time to be your spouse's friend and do those little things for each other that build intimacy. And have a real happy marriage.

A GIRL IN CD STORE

There was once a guy who suffered from cancer... a cancer that can't be treated. He was 18 years old and he could die anytime. All his life, he was stuck in his house being taken cared by his mother. He never went outside but he was sick of staying home and wanted to go out for once. So he asked his mother and she gave him permission.

He walked down his block and found a lot of stores. He passed a CD store and looked through the front door for a second as he walked. He stopped and went back to look into the store. He saw a young girl about his age and he knew it was love at first sight. He opened the door and walked in, not looking at anything else but her. He walked closer and closer until he was finally at the front desk where she sat.

She looked up and asked, "Can I help you?"

She smiled and he thought it was the most beautiful smile he has ever seen before and wanted to kiss her right there.

He said, "Uh... Yeah... Umm... I would like to buy a CD."

He picked one out and gave her money for it.

"Would you like me to wrap it for you?" she asked, smiling her cute smile again.

He nodded and she went to the back.

She came back with the wrapped CD and gave it to him. He took it and walked out of the store. He went home and from then on, he went to that store every day and bought a CD, and she wrapped it for him. He took the CD home and put it in his closet. He was still too shy to ask her out and he really wanted to but he couldn't. His mother found out about this and told him to just ask her.

So the next day, he took all his courage and went to the store. He bought a CD like he did every day and once again she went to the back of the store and came back with it wrapped. He took it and when she wasn't looking, he left his phone number on the desk and ran out...

!!!RRRRRING!!!

The mother picked up the phone and said, "Hello?"

It was the girl!!! She asked for the boy and the mother started to cry and said, "You don't know? He passed away yesterday..."

The line was quiet except for the cries of the boy's mother. Later in the day. The mother went into the boy's room because she wanted to remember him. She thought she would start by looking at his clothes. So she opened the closet. She was face to face with piles and piles and piles of unopened CDs. She was surprised to find all those CDs and she picked one up and sat down on the bed and she started to open one.

Inside, there was a CD and as she took it out of the wrapper, out fell a piece of paper. The mother picked it up and started to read it.

It said: Hi... I think U R really cute. Do u wanna go out with me? Love, Jacelyn

The mother opened another CD...

Again there was a piece of paper. It said: Hi... I think U R really cute. Do u wanna go out with me? Love, Jacelyn. Love is... when you've had a huge fight but then decide to put aside your egos, hold hands and say, "I Love You"

IMPORTANT THAN PRESENTS

A man going abroad to work leaves his fiancée crying. "Don't worry, I will write you every day," he said. For years he did write her. But since he was happy with his job, he had no immediate plans of going home. One day, he received a wedding invitation. His girlfriend was scheduled to be married. To whom? To the mailman bringing regularly the letters of her boy friend! Indeed, distance does make hearts flounder.

The poor boyfriend surely explained, "What went wrong? I sent her letters, chocolates, and flowers." When relationships go wrong, the list of things given and done for the person usually crops up. We say, "I have given you this and that...I have done these things for you." It seems that love is simply proven by the bestowal of gifts and favors.

But while presents are important, love demands what is basic: presence of the beloved. I have observed for instance, the orchids of my mother.

When she's away for a long time, they are unhealthy and many of them wither. But when she is around, they bloom with beautiful flowers. My mother does nothing exceptional. She just spends much time talking and caressing them.

I guess persons all the more require a caring presence. Love is fundamentally a commitment to a person. We may be committed to our business, job, hobby, sports and clubs, but strictly speaking, they cannot love us back. Only a person can love us in return, and for that matter the highest commitment as human beings is spending time with those persons we love.

And since people need affection and nourishment, material things can only help up to a certain degree in fostering love. But it can never replace the greatest gift of presence.

Martha was busy with her job. She believed

she had to work harder because she loves her father who is sick of cancer. She has to provide for his expensive medicines. Her brothers and sisters meanwhile stayed with their father most of the time. They bathed him, sang for him, spoon-fed him or simply kept him company.

One day Martha was hurt. She overheard her father telling her mother, "All our children love me except Martha." "How can this be?" Martha thought. "Am I not the one killing myself in my work to have money to buy for his medicines? My brothers and sisters do not even provide their share in the expenses as much as I do."

One night, as Martha was as usual late in

going home, she peeped for the first time in the room where her father was lying. She noticed that her father was still awake. She decided to come close at his bedside. Her father held her hands and said, "I miss you. I don't have much time. Stay with me." And she stayed with her father holding his hand the whole night. The next morning Martha said to everybody, "I have taken a leave of absence. I would like to be with father. I will bathe him and sing for him from now on." Her father had a beautiful smile. He knew this time Martha loves him.

* As children, we need the assuring presence of our loved ones. Adult people need no less. *

THE PERFECT GIFT

It's just a small, white envelope stuck among the branches of our Christmas tree. No name, no identification, no inscription. It has peeked through the branches of our tree at this time of the year for the past 10 years or so. It all began because my husband Mike hated Christmas. Oh, not the true meaning of Christmas, but the commercial aspects of it. You know, the overspending, the frantic running around at the last minute to get a tie for Uncle Harry and the dusting powder for Grandma, the gifts given in desperation because you couldn't think of anything else.

Knowing he felt this way, I decided one year to bypass the usual shirts, sweaters, ties and so forth. I reached for something special just for Mike. The inspiration came in an unusual way. Our son Kevin, who was 12 that year, was wrestling at the junior level at the school he attended. Shortly before Christmas, there was a non-league match against a team sponsored by an inner city church. The kids were mostly black.

These youngsters, dressed in sneakers so ragged that shoestrings seemed to be the only thing holding them together, presented a sharp contrast to our boys in their spiffy blue and gold uniforms and sparkling new wrestling shoes.

As the match began, I was alarmed to see that the other team was wrestling without head gear, a kind of light helmet designed to protect a wrestler's ears. It was a luxury the ragtag team obviously couldn't afford. Well, we ended up walloping them. We took every weight class. And as each of their boys got up from the mat, he swaggered around in his tatters with false bravado, a kind of street pride that couldn't acknowledge defeat.

Mike, seated beside me, shook his head sadly, "I wish just one of them could have won," he said. "They have a lot of potential, but losing like this could take the heart right out of them." Mike loved kids-all kids. He understood kids in competitive situations, having coached little league football, baseball and lacrosse. That's when the idea for his present came. That afternoon, I went to a local sporting goods store and bought an assortment of wrestling headgear and shoes and sent them anonymously to the inner city church. On Christmas Eve, I placed the envelope on the tree, the note inside telling Mike what I had done and that this was his gift from me. His smile was the brightest thing about Christmas that year and in succeeding years. For each Christmas, I followed the tradition - one year sending a group of mentally challenged youngsters to a hockey game, another year a check to a pair of elderly brothers whose home had burned to the ground the week before Christmas - on and on... The envelope became the highlight of our Christmas. It was always the last thing opened on Christmas morning and our children, ignoring their new toys, would stand with wide-eyed anticipation as their dad lifted the envelope from the tree to reveal its contents. As the children grew, the toys gave way to more practical presents, but the envelope never lost its allure. Still, the story doesn't end there. You see, we lost Mike last year due to cancer.

When Christmas rolled around, I was still so wrapped in grief that I barely got the tree up. Yet Christmas Eve found me placing an envelope on the tree, and in the morning, it was joined by three more. Each of our children, unbeknownst to the others, had placed an envelope on the tree for their dad.

The tradition has grown and someday will expand even further, with our grandchildren standing around the tree with wide-eyed anticipation, watching as their fathers take down their envelopes. Mike's spirit, like the spirit of Christmas, will always be with us.

POISON

A long time ago, a girl named Li-Li got married and went to live with her husband and mother-in-law. In a very short time, Li-Li found that she couldn't get along with her mother-in-law at all. Their personalities were very different, and Li-Li was angered by many of her mother-in-law's habits. In addition, she criticized Li-Li constantly.

Days passed days, and weeks passed weeks. Li-Li and her mother-in-law never stopped arguing and fighting. But what made the situation even worse was that, according to ancient Chinese tradition, Li-Li had to bow to her mother-in-law and obey her every wish. All the anger and unhappiness in the house was causing the poor husband great distress. Finally, Li-Li could not stand her mother-in-law's bad temper and dictatorship any longer, and she decided to do something about it. Li-Li went to see her father's good friend, Mr. Huang, who sold herbs. She told him the situation and asked if he would give her some poison so that she could solve the problem once and for all. Mr. Huang thought for a while, and finally said, Li-Li, I will help you solve your problem, but you must listen to me and obey what I tell you. Li-Li said, "Yes, Mr. Huang, I will do whatever you tell me to do." Mr. Huang went into the back room, and returned in a few minutes with a package of herbs. He told Li-Li, "You can't use a quick-acting poison to get rid of your mother-in-law, because that would cause people to become suspicious. Therefore, I have given you a number of herbs that will slowly build up poison in her body. Every other day prepare some pork or chicken and put a little of these herbs in her serving. Now, in order to make sure that nobody suspects you when she dies, you must be very careful to act very friendly towards her. Don't argue with her, obey her every wish, and treat her like a queen." Li-Li was so happy. She thanked Mr. Huang and hurried home to start her plot of murdering her mother-in-law.

Weeks went by, and months went by, and every other day, Li-Li served the specially treated food to her mother-in-law. She remembered what Mr. Huang had said about avoiding suspicion, so she controlled her temper, obeyed her mother-in-law, and treated her like her own mother. After six months had passed, the whole household had changed. Li-Li had practiced controlling her temper so much that she found that she almost never got mad or upset. She hadn't had an argument in six months with her mother-in-law, who now seemed much kinder and easier to get along with.

The mother-in-law's attitude toward Li-Li changed, and she began to love Li-Li like her own daughter. She kept telling friends and relatives that Li-Li was the best daughter-in-law one could ever find. Li-Li and her mother-in-law were now treating each other like a real mother and daughter. Li-Li's husband was very happy to see what was happening. One day, Li-Li came to see Mr. Huang and asked for his help again. She said, "Dear Mr. Huang, please help me to keep the poison from killing my mother-in-law! She's changed into such a nice woman, and I love her like my own mother. I do not want her to die because of the poison I gave her." Mr. Huang smiled and nodded his head. "Li-Li, there's nothing to worry about. I never gave you any poison. The herbs I gave you were vitamins to improve her health. The only poison was in your mind and your attitude toward her, but that has been all washed away by the love which you gave to her." MORAL: Friends, have you ever realized that how you treat others is exactly how they will treat you? In China it is said: The person who loves others will also be loved. THE GOLDEN RULE

THE TENDER CARESS

Michael and I did not know when the waiter put the plates on our table. At the time we were sitting in a small restaurant, hidden from the busy Third Street, in New York City. Even the smell of fresh serving blintze did not interfere with our conversation. In fact, we let the blintze soaked in the sour cream. We just enjoy the conversation too much that we forgot to eat. Our conversation was so delighted though we did not speak about important things. We laughing and speaking about the movie which we have just watched the night before and arguing about the meaning in our literature seminar. He told me about the maturity step to adulthood when he only responded if someone called him "Michael" and pretend not to hear if they called him "Mikey". Was that at the age 12 or 14? He did not remember but he recalled his mother cried and said that he became a man too fast. When we tasted the blueberry blintzes, i told him that my brother and i used to pick wild blueberry when visiting our cousins in the farm. I remembered i always finished ate my share before we went home and my aunt always warning i must be had a stomachache. But of course, it never happened.

While our fun conversation continued, my eyes went across the room and stop on the corner. A couple of old folks sit in there. The woman wearing the flower dress with faded color, the same with the pillow where she laid her pallid handbag. The man's top head shined just like the boiled egg which he ate very slowly. The woman chewed her oatmeal very slowly too, seemed with very much much effort.

But what made my mind thought about them was the silence around them. It seemed like the melancholy emptiness filled their corner. When our conversation became the whisper, from the confession to judges, the silence of the couple disturbed me. How sadden, I thought, if there was nothing at all to talk about. Was there any pages in each other's life they had not read? How if it happened to us?

Michael and I paid our food and went on. When we passed the corner where the couple sat, my wallet fallen. When I stooped to get it, I saw, under the table, they were tenderly holding each other's hand. They were eating in silence while holding each other's hand! I stood upright.

I was very touched to see the simple yet the very meaningful action reflecting the close relationship of the couple. I felt special allowing to watch it. The tender caress the old man's hand to his wife's wrinkle and tired fingers, filled, not only what i though was an empty corner, but it filled my heart too. Their silence was not the uncomfortable emptiness like the one we used to have after the jokes we had on our first date. It was not that. Their silence was the pleasant and relaxing one, it was the expression of the tender love and it did not always need the words to express it. They might spent the hours like these in the morning. Maybe this morning was no different from yesterday, but they enjoyed it with peace. They receiving their partner for what they are.

When I and Michael out of the restaurant, I thought, maybe it was nothing bad at all if some day we have something like that. Maybe, it will become the expression of the tender and complete love.

MAKING RELATIONS SPECIAL

When I was a kid, my Mom liked to make breakfast food for dinner every now and then. And I remember one night in particular when she had made dinner after a long, hard day at work. On that evening so long ago, my Mom placed a plate of eggs, sausage and extremely burned biscuits in front of my dad. I remember waiting to see if anyone noticed! Yet all dad did was reached for his biscuit, smile at my Mom and ask me how my day was at school.

I don't remember what I told him that night, but I do remember watching him smear butter and jelly on that biscuit and eat every bite! When I got up from the table that evening, I remember hearing my Mom apologize to my dad for burning the biscuits. And I'll never forget what he said: "Honey, I love burned biscuits."

Later that night, I went to kiss Daddy good night and I asked him if he really liked his biscuits burned. He wrapped me in his arms and said, "Your Momma put in a hard day at work today and she's real tired. And besides – a little burned biscuit never hurt anyone!"

Moral: Life is full of imperfect things and imperfect people. I'm not the best at hardly anything, and I forget birthdays and anniversaries just like everyone else.

But what I've learned over the years is that learning to accept each other's faults – and choosing to celebrate each other's differences – is one of the most important keys to creating a healthy, growing, and lasting relationship.

FATHER SON CONVERSATION

Once day, father was doing some work and his son came and asked, "Daddy, may I ask you a question?" Father said, "Yeah sure, what it is?" So his son asked, "Dad, how much do you make an hour?" Father got bit upset and said, "That's none of your business. Why do you ask such a thing?" Son said, "I just want to know. Please tell me, how much do you make an hour?" So, father told him that "I make Rs. 500 per hour."

"Oh", the little boy replied, with his head down. Looking up, he said, "Dad, may I please borrow Rs. 300?" The father furiously said, "if the only reason you asked about my pay is so that you can borrow some money to buy a silly toy or other nonsense, then march yourself to your room and go to bed. Think why you are being so selfish. I work hard every day and do not like this childish behavior."

The little boy quietly went to his room and shut the door. The man sat down and started to get even angrier about the little boy's questions. How dare he ask such questions only to get some money? After about an hour or so, the man had calmed down, and started to think, "May be there was something he really needed to buy with that Rs. 300 and he really didn't ask for money very often!" The man went to the door of little boy's room and opened the door. "Are you a sleep, son?" He asked. "No daddy, I'm awake," replied the boy. "I've been thinking, maybe I was too hard on you earlier", said the man. "It's been a long day and I took out my aggravation on you, Here's the Rs.300 you asked for".

The little boy sat straight up, smiling "oh thank you dad!" He yelled. Then, reaching under his pillow he pulled some crippled up notes. The man, seeing that the boy already had money, started to get angry again. The little boy slowly counted out his money, then looked up at his father.

"Why do you want money if you already had some?" the father grumbled. "Because I didn't have enough, but now I do," the little boy replied. "Daddy I have Rs. 500 now. Can I buy an hour of your time? Please come home early tomorrow. I would like to have dinner with you". Father was dumbstruck.

Moral: It's just a short reminder to all of you working so hard in life! We should not let time slip through our fingers without having spent some time with those who really matter to us, those close to our hearts. If we die tomorrow, the company that we are working for could easily replace us in a matter of days. But the family & friends we leave behind will feel the loss for the rest of their lives. And come to think of it, we pour ourselves more into work than to our family.

GRANDPA'S TABLE DINNER

A frail old man went to live with his son, daughter-in- law, and four-year old grandson. The old man's hands trembled, his eyesight was blurred, and his step faltered. The family ate together at the table. But the elderly Grandfather's shaky hands and failing sight made eating difficult. Peas rolled off his spoon onto the floor. When he grasped, the glass, milk spilled on the tablecloth.

The son and daughter-in- law became irritated with the mess. "We must do something about Grandfather," said the son. "I've had enough of his spilled milk, noisy eating, and food on the floor." So the husband and wife set a small table in the corner. There, Grandfather ate alone while the rest of the family enjoyed dinner. Since Grandfather had broken a dish or two, his food was served in a wooden bowl. When the family glanced in Grandfather' s direction, sometimes he had a tear in his eye as he sat alone. Still, the only words the couple had for him were sharp admonitions when he dropped a fork or spilled food. The four-year-old watched it all in silence.

One evening before supper, the father noticed his son playing with wood scraps on the floor. He asked the child sweetly, "What are you making?" Just as sweetly, the boy responded, "Oh, I am making a little bowl for you and Mama to eat your food in when I grow up." The four-year-old smiled and went back to work. The words so struck the parents that they were speechless. Then tears started to stream down their cheeks. Though no word was spoken, both knew what must be done. That evening the husband took Grandfather's hand and gently led him back to the family table. For the remainder of his days he ate every meal with the family. And for some reason, neither husband nor wife seemed to care any longer when a fork was dropped, milk spilled, or the tablecloth soiled. Moral: Children are remarkably perceptive. Their eyes ever observe, their ears ever listen, and their minds ever process the messages they absorb. If they see us patiently provide a happy home atmosphere for family members, they will imitate that attitude for the rest of their lives. The wise parent realizes that every day the building blocks are being laid for the child's future. Let's be wise builders and role models. Because Children are our future. Life is about people connecting with people, and making a positive difference. Take care of yourself, and those you love, today, and every day!

ROSE FOR MOTHER

A man stopped at a flower shop to order some flowers to be wired to his mother who lived two hundred miles away. As he got out of his car he noticed a young girl sitting on the curb sobbing. He asked her what was wrong and she replied, "I wanted to buy a red rose for my mother. But I only have seventy-five cents, and a rose costs two dollars."

The man smiled and said, "Come on in with me. I'll buy you a rose." He bought the little girl her rose and ordered his own mother's flowers. As they were leaving he offered the girl a ride home. She said, "Yes, please! You can take me to my mother." She directed him to a cemetery, where she placed the rose on a freshly dug grave.

The man returned to the flower shop, canceled the wire order, picked up a bouquet and drove the two hundred miles to his mother's house.

Moral: Life is Short. Spend much time as you can loving and caring people who love you. Enjoy each moment with them before it's too late. There is nothing important than family.

A SOLDIER'S STORY

A story is told about a soldier who was finally coming home after having fought in Vietnam. He called his parents from San

Francisco. "Mom and Dad, I'm coming home, but I've a favor to ask. I have a friend I'd like to bring home with me. "Sure," they replied, "we'd love to meet him." "There's something you should know," the son continued, "he was hurt pretty badly in the fighting. He stepped on a land mind and lost an arm and a leg. He has nowhere else to go, and I want him to come live with us."

"I'm sorry to hear that, son. Maybe we can help him find somewhere to live."

"No, Mom and Dad, I want him to live with us." "Son," said the father, "you don't know what you're asking. Someone with such a handicap would be a terrible burden on us. We have our own lives to live, and we can't let something like this interfere with our lives. I think you should just come home and forget about this guy. He'll find a way to live on his own."

At that point, the son hung up the phone. The parents heard nothing more from him. A few days later, however, they received a call from the San Francisco police. Their son had died after falling from a building, they were told. The police believed it was suicide.

The grief-stricken parents flew to San Francisco and were taken to the city morgue to identify the body of their son. They recognized him, but to their horror they also discovered something they didn't know, their son had only one arm and one leg.

Moral: The parents in this story are like many of us. We find it easy to love those who are good-looking or fun to have around, but we don't like people who inconvenience us or make us feel uncomfortable. We would rather stay away from people who aren't as healthy, beautiful, or smart as we are. Thankfully, there's someone who won't treat us that way. Someone who loves us with an unconditional love that welcomes us into the forever family, regardless of how messed up we are. Tonight, before you tuck yourself in for the night, say a little prayer that God will give you the strength you need to accept people as they are, and to help us all be more understanding of those who are different from us!

GIFT FROM DAUGHTER

The story goes that some time ago, a man punished his 3-year-old daughter for wasting a roll of gold wrapping paper. Money was tight and he became infuriated when the child tried to decorate a box to put under the Christmas tree. Nevertheless, the little girl brought the gift to her father the next morning and said, "This is for you, Daddy." The man was embarrassed by his earlier overreaction, but his anger flared again when he found out the box was empty. He yelled at her, stating, "Don't you know, when you give someone a present, there is supposed to be something inside? The little girl looked up at him with tears in her eyes and cried, "Oh,

Daddy, it's not empty at all. I blew kisses into the box. They're all for you, Daddy." The father was crushed. He put his arms around his little girl, and he begged for her forgiveness. Only a short time later, an accident took the life of the child. It is also told that her father kept that gold box by his bed for many years and, whenever he was discouraged, he would take out an imaginary kiss and remember the love of the child who had put it there. **Moral:** In a very real sense, each one of us, as humans beings have been given a gold container filled with unconditional love from our children, family members, friends, and God. There is simply no other possession, anyone could hold, more precious than this.

OLD MAN AND HIS SON

An old man lived alone in Minnesota. He wanted to spade his potato garden, but it was very hard work. His only son, who would have helped him, was in prison. The old man wrote a letter to his son and mentioned his situation:

Dear Son, I am feeling pretty bad because it looks like I won't be able to plant my potato garden this year. I hate to miss doing the garden because your mother always loved planting time. I'm just getting too old to be digging up a garden plot. If you were here, all my troubles would be over. I know you would dig the plot for me, if you weren't in prison. Love, Dad

Shortly, the old man received this telegram: 'For Heaven's sake, Dad, don't dig up the garden!! That's where I buried the GUNS!!' At 4 a.m. the next morning, a dozen FBI agents and local police officers showed up and dug up the entire garden without finding any guns. Confused, the old man wrote another note to his son telling him what had happened, and asked him what to do next. His son's reply was: 'Go ahead and plant your potatoes, Dad. It's the best I could do for you, from here.'

Moral: No Matter where you are in the World, if you have decided to do something deep from your heart, you can do it. It is the thought that matters, not where you are or where the person is.

THE ARMY SON

The Creighton's were very proud of their son, Frank. When he went to college, naturally they missed him; but he wrote and they looked forward to his letters and saw him on weekends. Then Frank was drafted into the army.

After he had been in the army about five months, he received his call to go to Vietnam. Of course, the parents' anxiety for his first letter was greater than ever before. And every week they heard from him and were thankful for his well-being. Then one week went by without a letter ~ two weeks ~ and finally three. At the end of the third week a telegram came, saying, "We regret to inform you that you son has been missing for three weeks and is presumed to have been killed inaction while fighting for his country." The parents were shocked and grieved. They tried to accept the situation and go on living, but it was tragically lonesome without Frank. About three weeks later, however, the phone rang. When Mrs. Creighton answered it, a voice on the other end said, "Mother, it's Frank. They found me, and I'm going to be all right. I'm in the United States and I'm coming home soon."Mrs. Creighton was overjoyed, with tears running down her cheeks she sobbed, "Oh, that's wonderful! That's just wonderful, Frank. "There was silence for a moment, and then Frank said, "Mother I want to ask you something that is important to me. While I've been here, I've met a lot of wonderful people and I've really become close friends with some. There is one fellow I would like to bring home with me to meet you and Dad. And I would like to know if it would be all right if he could stay and live with us, because he has no place to go ."His mother assured him it would be all right.

Then Frank said, "You see, he wasn't' as lucky as some; he was injured in battle. He was hit by a blast and his face is all disfigured. He lost his leg, and his right hand is missing. So you see, he feels uneasy about how others will accept him."

Frank's mother stopped to think a minute. She began to wonder how things would work out, and what people in town would think of someone like that. She said, "Sure frank, you bring him home~ for a visit, that is. We would love to meet him and have him stay for a while; but about him staying with us permanently, well, we'll have to think about that." There was silence for a minute, and then Frank said, "Okay, Mother," and hung up. A week went by without any word from Frank, and then a telegram arrived ~ "We regret to inform you that your son has taken his life. We would like you to come and identify the body. "Their wonderful son was gone. The horror stricken parents could only ask themselves, "Why had he done this?" When they walked into the room to identify the body of their son, they found a young man with a disfigured face, one leg missing, and his right hand gone.

DOG AND CAT

I just realized that while children are dogs -- loyal and affectionate -- teenagers are cats. It's so easy to be a dog owner. You feed it, train it, boss it around. It puts its head on your knee and gazes at you as if you were a Rembrandt painting. It bounds indoors with enthusiasm when you call it.

Then around age 13, your adoring little puppy turns into a big old cat. When you tell it to come inside, it looks amazed, as if wondering who died and made you emperor.

Instead of dogging your doorsteps, it disappears. You won't see it again until it gets hungry -- then it pauses on its sprint through the kitchen long enough to turn its nose up at whatever you're serving. When you reach out to ruffle its head, in that old affectionate gesture, it twists away from you, then gives you a blank stare, as if trying to remember where it has seen you before.

You, not realizing that the dog is now a cat, think something must be desperately wrong with it. It seems so antisocial, so distant, sort of depressed. It won't go on family outings.

Since you're the one who raised it, taught it to fetch and stay and sit on command, you assume that you did something wrong. Flooded with guilt and fear, you redouble your efforts to make your pet behave.

Only now you're dealing with a cat, so everything that worked before now produces the opposite of the desired result. Call it, and it runs away. Tell it to sit, and it jumps on the counter. The more you go toward it, wringing your hands, the more it moves away. Instead of continuing to act like a dog owner, you can learn to behave like a cat owner. Put a dish of food near the door, and let it come to you. But remember that a cat needs your help and your affection too. Sit still, and it will come, seeking that warm, comforting lap it has not entirely forgotten. Be there to open the door for it. One day your grown-up child will walk into the kitchen, give you a big kiss and say, "You've been on your feet all day. Let me get those dishes for you." Then you'll realize your cat is a dog again.

USELESS LIFE

A farmer got so old that he couldn't work the fields anymore. So he would spend the day just sitting on the porch. His son, still working the farm, would look up from time to time and see his father sitting there. "He's of no use any more," the son thought to himself, "he doesn't do anything!"

One day the son got so frustrated by this, that he built a wood coffin, dragged it over to the porch, and told his father to get in. Without saying anything, the father climbed inside. After closing the lid, the son dragged the coffin to the edge of the farm where there was a high cliff. As he approached the drop, he heard a light tapping on the lid from inside the coffin. He opened it up.

Still lying there peacefully, the father looked up at his son. "I know you are going to throw me over the cliff, but before you do, may I suggest something?" "What is it?" replied the son. "Throw me over the cliff, if you like," said the father, "but save this good wood coffin. Your children might need to use it."

TWO SEEDS:

Two seeds lay side by side in the fertile soil.

The first seed said, "I want to grow! I want to send my roots deep into the soil beneath me, and thrust my sprouts through the earth's crust above me ... I want to unfurl my tender buds like banners to announce the arrival of spring ... I want to feel the warmth of the sun on my face and the blessing of the morning dew on my petals!"

And so she grew...

The second seed said, "Hmmmm. If I send my roots into the ground below, I don't know what I will encounter in the dark. If I push my way through the hard soil above me I may damage my delicate sprouts ... what if I let my buds open and a snail tries to eat them? And if I were to open my blossoms, a small child may pull me from the ground. No, it is much better for me to wait until it is safe."

And so she waited... A yard hen scratching around in the early spring ground for food found the waiting seed and promptly ate it.

DESIRE.

If the things you desire are only for yourself, then what you accomplish will be empty and unfulfilling. Desire turned inward is nothing but greed, and will bring you nothing worth having. The greediest people are not those who desire too much. The greediest people are those who desire too little, who desire only for their own narrow, limited concerns.

The more outwardly your desires are focused, the more fulfilling will the fruits of those desires be. What you desire for the world beyond you, for all of life itself, will bring the most lasting, fulfilling rewards. The person who solves his own small problems will receive some real value from his efforts.

Yet when that person can make the same innovation available to others, the value that can be created is virtually unlimited. Desire can be a powerful force, so be sure to point it in a positive direction. The more your desire is focused beyond your own concerns, the further it will take you and your world.

A MOST IMPORTANT LESSON

During my second month of nursing school, our professor gave us a pop quiz. I was a conscientious student and had breezed through the questions, until I read the last one: "What is the first name of the woman who cleans the school?" Surely, this was some kind of joke. I had seen the cleaning woman several times. She was tall, dark-haired and in her 50s, but how would I know her name? I handed in my paper, leaving the last question blank.

Just before class ended, one student asked if the last question would count toward our quiz grade. "Absolutely," said the professor. "In your careers, you will meet many people. All are significant. They deserve your attention and care, even if all you do is smile and say 'hello'." "I've never forgotten that lesson. I also learned her name was Dorothy

BLURRED VISION

A businessman was highly critical of his competitors' storefront windows. "Why, they are the dirtiest windows in town," he claimed. Fellow business people grew tired of the man's continual criticism and nitpicking comments about the windows. One day over coffee, the businessman carried the subject just too far. Before leaving, a fellow store owner suggested the man get his own windows washed. He followed the advice, and the next day at coffee, he exclaimed, "I can't believe it. As soon as I washed my windows, my competitor must have cleaned his too. You should see them shine."

Confucius once declared, "Don't complain about the snow on your neighbor's roof when your own doorstep is unclean."

DON'T CHANGE THE WORLD

Once upon a time, there was a king who ruled a prosperous country. One day, he went for a trip to some distant areas of his country. When he was back to his palace, he complained that his feet were very painful, because it was the first time that he went for such a long trip, and the road that he went through was very rough and stony. He then ordered his people to cover every road of the entire country with leather. Definitely, this would need thousands of cows' skin, and would cost a huge amount of money. Then one of his wise servants dared himself to tell the king, "Why do you have to spend that unnecessary amount of money? Why don't you just cut a little piece of leather to cover your feet?" The king was surprised, but he later agreed to his suggestion, to make a "shoe" for himself. There is actually a valuable lesson of life in this story: to make this world a happy place to live, you better change yourself - your heart; and not the world.

A PAIR OF SHOES

When I got sober my sponsor told me that I had to be willing to change everything about my life -- everything. So, I wore blue jeans and switched to slacks. I wore western shirts and switched to T-shirts. But the one thing I just couldn't give up was my cowboy boots.

I went to my sponsor and said, "Surely I won't get drunk over a silly pair of cowboy boots. I'm willing to change a lot of things, and if needed I could even give up those boots, but it seems so silly."

My sponsor said, "I don't know how silly it is, or if you'll get drunk over those cowboy boots, but I can tell that you are not 'entirely' willing, though."

"Okay, okay," I said. "I'll prove it to you. I'll give up the boots for 30 days just to demonstrate my willingness to God."

So, I bought a pair of tennis shoes, and after 30 days of not wearing my cowboy boots, wearing tennis shoes instead, the strangest thing happened -- my feet stopped hurting.

That's how it was getting sober and giving up the high life. I never stopped to think that the boots were causing my feet to hurt, or the booze was causing my life to hurt. I got willing to give up the stuff, one day at a time, for 30 days, then 60 days, then 90 days ... and my life stopped hurting.

And every day I do something different, some change in some small way. Maybe I just put my socks on different, or drive to work a new way. Every day, I try to do Little Things in a Big Way so that when Big Things happen I can handle them in a Little Way.

OLD WEST JUSTICE

A man in the Old West was being tried for stealing a horse. You need to remember that stealing a horse in the Old West was a very grave and serious offense. A person could be hanged if found guilty of such a deed.

It so happened that the man whose horse had been stolen had always made it a point to get the best of any person with whom he had any dealings. He had never tried to do anything good for anyone other than himself. Consequently, the man whose horse had been stolen didn't have a single friend in the entire town. The case was tried and presented to the jury. The evidence against the accused man was pretty strong. After about thirty minutes of deliberation, the jury returned to the court chambers. "Gentlemen of the jury, have you reached a verdict?" The judge asked. The chairman of the jury stood up. "Yes we have, your honor," he replied. "What is your verdict?" inquired the judge. There were a few moments of silence and then the chairman spoke. "We find the defendant not guilty if he will return the horse." After the judge had silenced the laughter in the courtroom, he admonished the jury. "I cannot accept that verdict. You will have to retire until you reach another verdict," said the judge. The jury went back into their room to deliberate toward another verdict. No member of the jury had any particular liking for the man whose horse had been stolen. At one time or another he had gotten the best of each of them. About an hour passed before the jury could reach another verdict. They re-entered the courtroom. They took their place in the jury box and the courtroom grew silent. "Gentlemen of the jury," began the judge, "have you reached a verdict?" The chairman of the jury stood up.

"Yes we have, your honor," he replied. "What is your verdict?" asked the judge.

The courtroom was totally silent. You could have heard a pin drop. Everyone eagerly awaited the verdict. The chairman read the decision reached by the twelve good men, tried and true. "We find the defendant not guilty, and he can keep the horse!"
The courtroom burst into laughter!

Moral of the story: If you spend your life trying to take advantage of others, never caring about them in any way except what you can get from them or what they can do for you, you will end up a loser, like the man who lost his horse. If you desire a friend, then be a friend. If you desire for other people to help you, then help other people. If you desire justice at the hands of others, then practice justice toward them. Regardless of what you may think, the old Biblical admonition is true. We do reap what we sow.

FATHER AND HIS SONS

A father had a family of sons who were perpetually quarreling among themselves. When he failed to heal their disputes by his exhortations, he determined to give them a practical illustration of the evils of disunion; and for this purpose he one day told them to bring him a bundle of sticks. When they had done so, he placed the faggot into the hands of each of them in succession, and ordered them to break it in pieces. They tried with all their strength, and were not able to do it. He next opened the faggot, took the sticks separately, one by one, and again put them into his sons' hands, upon which they broke them easily. He then addressed them in these words: "My sons, if you are of one mind, and unite to assist each other, you will be as this faggot, uninjured by all the attempts of your enemies; but if you are divided among yourselves, you will be broken as easily as these sticks."

THE LESSON OF THE HOMELESS

It was a cold winter's day that Sunday. The parking lot to the church was filling up quickly. I noticed as I got out of my car fellow church members were whispering among themselves as they walked in the church. As I got closer I saw a man leaned up against the wall outside the church. He was almost lying down as if he was asleep. He had on a long trench coat that was almost in shreds and a hat topped his head, pulled down so you could not see his face. He wore shoes that looked 30 years old, too small for his feet, with holes all over them, his toes stuck out. I assumed this man was homeless, and asleep, so I walked on by through the doors of the church. We all fellowshipped for a few minutes, and someone brought up the man lying outside. People snickered and gossiped but no one bothered to ask him to come in, including me. A few moments later church began. We all waited for the Preacher to take his place and to give us the Word, when the doors to the church opened. In came the homeless man walking down the aisle with his head down. People gasped and whispered and made faces. He made his way down the aisle and up onto the pulpit where he took off his hat and coat. My heart sank. There stood our preacher...he was the "homeless man."

No one said a word. The preacher took his Bible and laid it on his stand. "Folks, I don't think I have to tell you what I am preaching about today. If you judge people, you have no time to love them."

FARMER FLEMING AND A NOBLEMAN

His name was Fleming, and he was a poor Scottish farmer. One day, while trying to eke out a living for his family, he heard a cry for help coming from a nearby bog. He dropped his tools and ran to the bog. There, mired to his waist in black muck, was a terrified boy, screaming and struggling to free himself. Farmer Fleming saved the lad from what could have been a slow and terrifying death. The next day, a fancy carriage pulled up to

the Scotsman's sparse surroundings. An elegantly dressed nobleman stepped out and introduced himself as the father of the boy Farmer Fleming had saved.
"I want to repay you," said the nobleman. "You saved my son's life."

"No, I can't accept payment for what I did," the Scottish farmer replied, waving off the offer.
At that moment, the farmer's own son came to the door of the family hovel. "Is that your son?" the nobleman asked.

"Yes," the farmer replied proudly.

"I'll make you a deal. Let me take him and

give him a good education. If the lad is anything like his father, he'll grow to a man you can be proud of."

And that he did. In time, Farmer Fleming's son graduated from St. Mary's Hospital Medical School in London, and went on to become known throughout the world as the noted Sir Alexander Fleming, the discoverer of Penicillin. Years afterward, the nobleman's son was stricken with pneumonia. What saved him? Penicillin. The name of the nobleman? Lord Randolph Churchill. His son's name? Sir Winston Churchill.

PAPERBACK BOOKS EDITED BY AUTHOR

Constantine-Simms has previously edited the following books:

- Rice & Peas For The Soul 2 (2015)
- Rice & Peas For The Soul 1 (2014)
- The Greatest Taboo: Homosexuality in Black Communities (2001)

- Hip Hop Had a Dream: Vol. 1 The Artful Movement (2008)
- 12 Years A Slave
- Behind The Scenes
- Thirty Years A Slave,...
- Incidents in the Life of a Slave...
- Fifty Years In Chains
- From Bondage To Freedom
- Hearts and Minds (Vol. 1)

- Hearts and Minds (Vol. 2)

E-BOOKS BY AUTHOR

- How to Get Motivated
- How to Plan For A New Career
- How to Develop Unstoppable Confidence
- Successful Interviews: Making The Most Of The Interview
- The Interview Guide: A Job Interview Is No Different Than Finding The Right Partner
- The Structure and Application of Cognitive Behavioural Therapy
- How to Think Critically
- Mentoring As A Workforce Development Strategy
- The Counselling Process In Six Stages: A Basic Guide For Psychologists Counsellors

and Psychotherapists

- Linking Emotional Intelligence To Effective Leadership
- Stress Management
- A Critique Of Executive Coaching Through The Psychodynamic Window
- Otto Kernberg's Theory of Personality: Pathological Narcissism and Borderline Personality Disorders
- Personality Development and Confidence Building
- The Psychology of the Courtroom
- How To Improve Your Communication Skills
- How Employment Assessment Centres Work
- Effective Presentations Skills
- Linking Emotional Intelligence To Effective Leadership

- Stress Management Leading Career Development and Employability
- The History of Psychological Testing
- How To Have A Bad Interview
- Have You Ever Thought of Becoming A Life Coach
- Successful Interviews
- The 360 Degree Feedback System Is By Far The Best Performance Assessment Tool By Far.

www.ingramcontent.com/pod-product-compliance
Ingram Content Group UK Ltd.
Pitfield, Milton Keynes, MK11 3LW, UK
UKHW020417250726
13967UKWH00007B/2690

9 781631 733154